Golden Highlights Library

Great Cathedrals

Frederick Cheam

Golden Press

Published in 1974 by **Golden Press, New York,**
a division of Western Publishing Company, Inc.
Library of Congress Catalog Card Number: 73–87968

Created, designed and produced for
Western Publishing Company, Inc. by
Trewin Copplestone Publishing Ltd, London

Printed in Italy by
Officine Grafiche Arnoldo Mondadori, Verona
Filmset by Photoprint Plates Ltd, Rayleigh, Essex
World rights reserved by
Western Publishing Company, Inc.
GOLDEN and GOLDEN PRESS ® are trademarks
of Western Publishing Company, Inc.

ISBN: 0 307 43120 7

Contents

Acknowledgments

Aerofilms, London 27t; Alinari 7; Alinari/Giraudon
39b; J. Allan Cash 38, 39t; Archives Photographiques
54t, 55; Bavaria Verlag 8, 13; State Museum, Berlin–
Dahlem 66; British Tourist Authority 14b, 27b, 31;
Burkhard-Verlag 25; Colorific 77t; Trewin
Copplestone 65; Courtauld Institute of Art 47b, 73;
Michael Dyer Associates 4, 34–5; Elsam, Mann &
Cooper Ltd 78; French Tourist Office 46; Giraudon
48t, 52r; Sonia Halliday 5, 29r, 32t, 45t, 52l; Hamlyn
Group Library 51l; Michael Holford 20t, b, 21, 29l,
33, 37t, 40, 45b, 68b; Alan Irvine 80; A. F. Kersting
10, 11l, r, 14b, 15, 16, 17, 18, 22l, r, 23, 26, 30l, 34l,
35r, 36, 37b, 42t, b, 43, 44, 47t, 49, 62, 63l, 67, 76t,
77b; Emily Lane 12, 32b, 48b; Mansell Collection 70,
71; MAS 63r; Douglas Mulquin 72b; National
Monuments Record 19, 74b, 75r; Phillips City
Studio 30r; Picturepoint 6, 28, 64, 72t, 79; Scala 9t,
b, 53, 60t, b, 61, 68t, 69; J. H. Schaefer & Son 76b;
Spectrum 40; ZFA 24, 56t.

Page 1 *Detail of the 13th-century stained glass of Canterbury Cathedral. The central roundel shows Christ appearing to Mary Magdalen.*

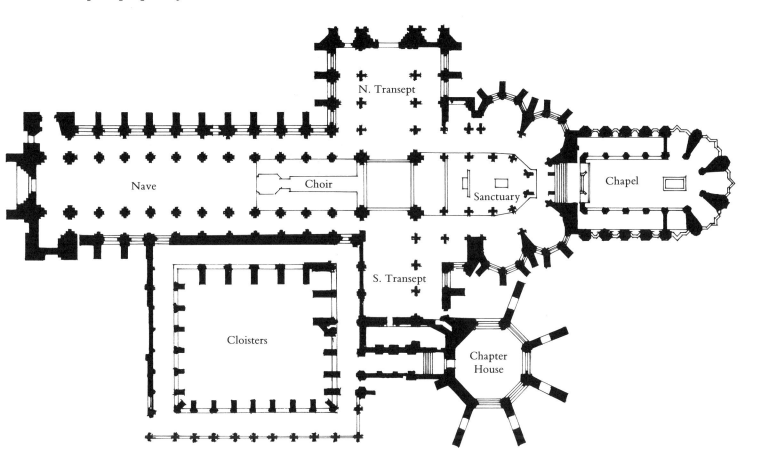

Plan of Westminster Abbey, London, showing the principal parts of a medieval cathedral.

N. Transept

Nave

Choir

Sanctuary

Chapel

Cloisters

S. Transept

Chapter House

Some Architectural Terms

CATHEDRALS can be enjoyed for all sorts of reasons–for their place in history, their associations, their religious significance, their picturesque charm. In this book they are looked at exclusively as architecture, and it therefore saves time and space to use a few terms that have specific architectural meanings.

A cathedral is the principal church of the diocese, containing the bishop's throne *(cathedra)*.

All cathedrals are divided into an eastern part (the **chancel** and **choir**) where the altar is situated and the clergy officiate, and a western part (the **nave**) which accommodates the congregation. Choir and chancel are usually a single unit architecturally and the words are used interchangeably. At the point where nave and chancel meet, **transepts** may project to north and south, all four arms meeting at the **crossing**, which may have a tower over it. Around the body of the church, at ground level, run **aisles**. The aisle around the choir is called the **ambulatory**; sometimes this is extended further east as a **retrochoir** ("behind the choir"). An **apse** is a semi-circular ending to any part of the building.

The **elevation** is the vertical face of the building, either inside or outside. The interior elevation of a cathedral usually consists of an **arcade** (i.e. a line of arches), a **gallery** and a **clerestory** ("clear story"), where windows can admit light above the level of the gallery roof. When the gallery is only a passage in the thickness of the wall it is called a **triforium**. The supports upon which the arches rest are called **piers**, and the space between one pier and the next is a **bay**.

A **vault** is a stone ceiling, usually curved in shape because it is built of a series of arches. A **tunnel vault** forms a continuous surface down the body of the church; a **groin vault** is formed by building bays in which two tunnel vaults meet at right angles, the edges being the groins; in a **rib vault** the groins are replaced by stone ribs which in theory act like a skeleton and support the **cells** in between. A **ridge-rib** goes down the whole crown of the vault; a **transverse rib** crosses the body of the church at right angles; a **diagonal rib** crosses from corner to corner of a bay. The point on the wall where the ribs begin is called the **springing**. A **tierceron** is a rib from springing to ridge-rib on either side of the diagonal; a **lierne** is a short rib joining any of the others.

3

Hagia Sophia, Istanbul

HAGIA SOPHIA, the Church of the Holy Wisdom, in Istanbul, is the oldest cathedral in the world, and apart from half-a-dozen basilicas in Rome, Ravenna and Bethlehem, the oldest large Christian church still standing. So it is a logical place to begin. Yet it is in some ways a false start, since both its structural system and its decoration belong to a style (the Byzantine) that was to have almost no influence on medieval and Renaissance architecture in the West, and the mainstream story of cathedral building has to begin all over again in the 11th century.

The Emperor Justinian commissioned Hagia Sophia in 532 to replace an earlier church destroyed by riots. His architects – Anthemius of Thralles and Isidore of Miletus – were both from Asia Minor, and they designed a building of vast size, great technical boldness and perfect proportions, a building for which, as far as we are aware, there was no precedent.

The structural system of Hagia Sophia is easy to grasp. It consists of a large square, defined by four huge corner piers. Four semi-circular arches connect these piers, and on them rests a shallow dome, penetrated all around its base by a ring of small windows. The transition from the square of the arches to the circle of the dome is made by concave triangles of masonry called pendentives, which fill the spaces. All this naturally weighs down upon the four main piers, pushing them outwards. They therefore have to be buttressed, and this is done in two ways. At the east and west ends the dome is abutted by smaller half-domes which are themselves held in position by yet smaller quarter-domes, transmitting the thrust in stages to the ground. At the north and south, massive masonry supports are placed directly against the piers. Inside the north and south arches, but not supporting them, are light screen-walls made up of a double arcade topped by two rows of windows, so that on these two sides are aisles and galleries.

Thus, in spite of the fact that the building is structurally a square, the main internal space (which includes the half-domes at each end but not the aisles and galleries) is twice as long as it is wide, and this is accentuated by a vestibule at the west end and an apsed choir at the east. The space, moreover, is treated with great subtlety. The screen walls beneath the quarter-domes are made concave in plan, so that the church seems to expand at each end. From the aisles and galleries, ever-changing cross views form as one moves through the building.

Left *Christ with Constantine IX (Monomachos) and the Empress Zoë, an 11th-century mosaic in one of the galleries of Hagia Sophia.*

Below *Hagia Sophia. The interior looking east, from a 19th-century lithograph. At this date the building was still being used as a mosque.*

Hagia Sophia, showing the two massive buttresses of the north side and the semi-dome of the east. The minarets are Turkish additions.

Justinian could call upon the resources of the whole empire to decorate his cathedral. The columns are of colored marble and the brick fabric of the walls is covered with marble veneer, giving the whole interior a palatial richness. Capitals and entablature, of white marble, are carved with stylized foliage patterns, smooth on the surface but deeply under cut behind, masterpieces of Byzantine craftsmanship. Finally, the upper walls were originally covered with glass mosaic. There are detailed descriptions of these mosaic pictures by the 6th-century writers Procopius and Paul the Silentiary, but hardly anything now survives from Justinian's time, and not much from later ages. Some may still lie hidden under the Ottoman whitewash. Procopius could hardly express the sense of wonder that the building

aroused, especially the radiant dome, with its corona of light. "It seems not to rest upon solid masonry, but to cover the space as though suspended by a golden chain from heaven."

The architects were indeed (like the builders of Beauvais, whom we shall meet later) too bold. The dome collapsed and had to be rebuilt at a steeper pitch, and throughout the centuries the buttressing on the north and south sides has had to be increased, resulting in the ungainly heaps of masonry which today make the exterior somewhat less than beautiful. Yet it remains a haunting building. After a thousand years of Christian worship, the last mass was held on May 28, 1453, after the armies of Sultan Mohammed II had already breached the walls of the city. From then until 1923 it was a mosque; it is now a public monument.

*St. Mark's, Venice. The interior looking from
the nave to the crossing, the iconostasis,
and beyond that the altar and* Pala d'Oro.

St. Mark's, Venice

ST. MARK'S, Venice, is an outpost of
Byzantine architecture in Europe. In the 11th
century Venice was building up the maritime
empire that was to make her one of the richest
of medieval cities, and the source of that wealth
was in the East. It was not surprising that the
Doges turned to Byzantine craftsmen when
they commissioned the church – or rather the
large private chapel – that was to hold the
relics of St. Mark, relics stolen from Alexandria
in the 9th century. It was not at that time the
seat of a bishop.

St. Mark's belongs to a type of church that
goes back at least as far as the Emperor
Justinian – a cross with four equal arms, each
covered by a dome, with a fifth dome in the
center, where the arms meet. Its plan thus
comes somewhere between the completely
unified space of Hagia Sophia and the standard
Romanesque plan of nave, choir and transepts
which we shall be examining in the next chapter. Though smaller and lower than Hagia
Sophia it contrives to be almost as rich in spatial
effect and, because it has survived as a living
church, it is perhaps even richer in emotional
impact. As at Hagia Sophia, the four main piers
are penetrated by arches at ground and gallery
levels; the aisles, which surround all the arms
of the church except that in the east, are not
roofed to form galleries but are left open to
the vault. What one calls galleries are only
narrow walks on the arcade wall itself, so that
as one threads one's way gingerly at this level a
series of dream-like spaces appear around one –
on all sides, above and below. The lighting is
dim, coming only from windows at the ends
of the arms and from small openings in the
domes. In the red glow of hanging lamps and
candles, the deep-colored marbles and spark-
ling golden mosaics create an impression of
cavernous mystery. At the heart of the mystery, partially hidden behind a stone screen
surmounted by statues of saints, stand the altar
and the shrine of St. Mark.

The western arm forms the nave, and this is surrounded on three sides by a passage forming a vestibule (or narthex) and baptistery. It too is mostly roofed with domes, much smaller than those inside but also covered in mosaics—the most interesting in the cathedral. Dating from the 13th century, they illustrate Old Testament stories from the Creation to the story of Joseph. The decoration of St. Mark's is, in fact, amazingly consistent. Much of the Byzantine furnishing survives, and the mosaics, in spite of being added to continuously for 400 years, still have a remarkable unity of style (post-Renaissance work is another matter: that is definitely obtrusive). One of the cathedral's greatest treasures, the *Pala d'Oro* (Golden Altar), goes back to the 11th century. It is made of small, brightly colored enamel plaques showing, against a gold background, saints and episodes from church history. After 1204 it was enlarged to incorporate new panels seized at Constantinople during the Fourth Crusade.

In 1095, when St. Mark's was finished, it probably looked almost as austere from outside as Hagia Sophia does today. It was the later Middle Ages which embellished it—some would say over-embellished it—with sculpture, pinnacles and frills of delicately carved stone. The loot of 1204 added more precious items of ornament, including the slab of porphyry showing emperors, and the four bronze horses high up on the façade—works of imperial Rome with a history longer than either Venice or Constantinople.

Left *Façade of St. Mark's. The four bronze horses are over the central door.*

Right *Part of the Pala d'Oro, made up of Byzantine enamels looted from Constantinople. Christ sits in the center, surrounded by the four Evangelists.*

Below *Detail of a mosaic from one of the small domes of the narthex, showing the creation of the birds and fishes.*

*Santiago de Compostela. The Romanesque nave
looking east towards the crossing.*

The 12th-century Pórtico de la Gloria. *The central column bears the imprint of a hand, worn into the stone by generations of pilgrims.*

The Baroque altar of Santiago. At the top Santiago himself (St. James) rides forth against the Moors.

Santiago de Compostela

THE Byzantine tradition continued in a few later buildings in Italy and France, and underwent strange transformations in Russia (pp. 64, 65), but for the mainstream of later cathedral architecture one must go to another source: the Early Christian basilica. Compared to the complexities of Hagia Sophia and St. Mark's, this is simplicity itself – a simple rectangular hall with an apse at the east end for the altar and a wide porch, or narthex, at the west. In order to admit light into it, the central part of the roof is raised up on a colonnade, thus creating a row of windows on each side (the clerestory), and dividing the interior into three parallel spaces, the nave in the middle and the aisles on either side. At the altar end there were often projections to north and south, the transepts, making the church plan into a T. This primitive basilican type is illustrated by old St. Peter's (p. 66) and the Lateran before it

was altered by Borromini in the 17th century.

The years between 500 and 1000 represent a period in which few large churches were built in the West, and from which none survive. Not until the 11th century was Christendom peaceful or powerful enough to turn its energies again to cathedrals, and the style which now emerged is that known as Romanesque. In the larger churches the basilican scheme was retained, but there were significant changes. The classical columns of the nave arcade have now become stout masonry piers, and they support a series of round arches, never a straight entablature. Between arcade and clerestory now runs a tall gallery, whose roof covers the aisle. The part cast of the transept has been lengthened and now accommodates the choir as well as the altar. The ceiling is sometimes of wood, as before, but increasingly often it is a vault, a semi-circular tunnel of stone resting on the clerestory walls Jand strengthened by thick transverse arches across the nave.

Santiago de Compostela owed its size and wealth to its claim to possession of the body of St. James the Great. Pilgrimages to his shrine began in the 9th century, and by the 11th had grown to be the most popular in Europe. Other towns through which the pilgrims passed *en route* for Santiago often held famous relics of their own, and a whole series of churches built to house them conform to the same pattern, the formula outlined above, except for one thing: they have no clerestories. In buildings of exceptional height and width the builders obviously lacked the confidence to rest their vaults on walls pierced by windows and only weakly buttressed on the outside.

Santiago was begun in 1077 and finished by about 1130. From the outside, the great church which still dominates the city gives little hint of its 11th-century core, but the inside is practically intact. Its plan is the one which will characterize almost all our cathedrals from now on – a cross with choir and nave running east–west and transepts north–south. Over the crossing rises a tower, with windows allowing light into the interior. Aisles go completely around the whole church, including the transepts, to facilitate the passage of pilgrims past the saint's shrine. Small apsidal chapels are added to the eastern side of the transepts and around the ambulatory.

The elevation and vaulting have already been sufficiently indicated. The total effect is one of stark grandeur. In spite of the absence of a clerestory the nave seems lofty, an impression helped by the vertical shafts rising uninterrupted from floor to vault and supporting the transverse arches. Sculpture is confined to the simple foliage capitals of the arcade and gallery.

The exterior presents a more complicated story, and a longer one. The original three façades, those of the west front and of the north and south transepts, were all richly decorated with sculpture. That of the north transept was completely rebuilt in the 18th century. That of the south, the *Puerta de las Platerías* or Door of the Silversmiths, so called because of the silversmiths' shops outside it, was for some reason altered soon after it was erected, preserving much of the sculpture but displacing it into a meaningless jumble; while the west front was rebuilt twice – once in the 12th century to install the *Pórtico de la Gloria* and again in the 18th, when this was hidden behind the present Baroque composition. Both the *Puerta de las Platerías* and the *Pórtico de la Gloria* are precious examples of their respective styles: the first of the urgent, still slightly naive period of around 1100; the second, carved between 1168 and 1188 by a master called Matthew, who may have been French, of the flowering early Gothic which we shall encounter again at Chartres.

Santiago cathedral is now so completely enclosed by later additions that it looks at first sight like a Baroque church. But the dominant features are still basically Romanesque – the central lantern tower, the tower attached to the south transept and the two towers of the west front. During the 18th century all were given their present exuberant upper parts. The west front, the *Obradoiro* ("work of gold"), forms one of the most splendid architectural sights in Spain. Built between 1738 and 1750 by Fernando Casas y Nova, and approached by a typically complicated arrangement of steps, its forms multiply as it rises, from the relatively austere columns flanking the main doorway and windows to the fantastic profusion of pinnacles, scrolls and gesticulating sculpture on the gable and the tops of the towers.

The Baroque west front of Santiago. Ornament and statuary are 18th century, but the two towers are Romanesque up to the level of the belfry.

13

The Chapel of the Nine Altars, Durham, looking north. Added in the 13th century, this forms a sort of extra transept behind the high altar.

The site of Durham is a fortress, a loop of the river Wear protected on three sides by steep cliffs, leaving only a narrow neck of land to the north, which was defended by the castle. The situation tells its own history. The first church here was built by monks from Lindisfarne, fleeing from Viking invaders in 875, seeking a place where they could live in safety and preserve their greatest relic, the body of St. Cuthbert. After the Norman Conquest, Durham, like many English monasteries, was made part of William's administrative system. The Benedictine Rule was introduced, and the Saxon abbot replaced by a Norman, who combined the office with that of bishop. These cathedral-monasteries are a peculiarly English institution. The bishop was nominally the head of the monastery, but he delegated his responsibilities to a prior. Clashes, sometimes violent, between bishop and prior are almost continuous throughout English ecclesiastical history, symbolized at Durham by the fact that the bishop lived in the castle, to the north of the cathedral, and the prior in his own apartments to the south of it.

Durham

IN the great wave of building activity that took place during the 11th century, the Romanesque style spread all over Europe. Master masons could move fairly freely from one country to another, so that technical or stylistic innovations quickly became common knowledge. Many of the characteristic qualities of Santiago–its largeness of scale, its cruciform plan, its stone vaults and its emphatic use of sculpture–are to be found in churches at opposite ends of Europe. At the same time, as was natural, separate regions evolved their own special brands of Romanesque. In France, particularly, contemporary buildings in Auvergne, Burgundy, Provence, Anjou or Normandy are easily distinguishable. The Romanesque of Normandy acquired a particular importance because it was carried over to England by William the Conqueror and became the style known in English architectural history as Norman. Of that style Durham is the supreme example.

The knocker on the north door of Durham. During the Middle Ages any fugitive who managed to grasp the handle could claim rights of sanctuary.

The so-called Galilee chapel of Durham, with its three-fold zigzags on the arches, is like the hall of a nobleman's palace in the 12th century.

The foundation stone of the present cathedral was laid on August 11, 1093, by Bishop William of St. Carileph. He was a Norman, and so, in all likelihood, was his master-mason, though by this time the Norman Romanesque style was naturalized English. The plan of the cathedral is the same as that of Santiago except that the transepts have aisles only on the east side; that is, they do not form a processional path right around the church. The interior elevation shows another important difference: instead of Santiago's two stories (arcade and gallery), Durham has a clerestory as well. Looking more closely, one notices another difference: the piers carrying the arcade are not all the same but alternate in form. One type consists of a cluster of small shafts, the other of a single round, fat column carved with an incised pattern—zig-zag, spiral or lozenge. The general impression is one of immense strength and solidity, but this variation in the piers has also a certain elegance that proclaims its designer's sophistication.

Looking up into the vault we see another,

even more important difference: rib vaults, destined to be one of the key features in the making of the Gothic style (see p. 28). Durham is the earliest building in Europe to use them on a major scale, and it is obvious enough that compared with later examples they are slightly awkward and experimental. Each bay is covered by a pair of diagonal semi-circular ribs, crossing in the middle. Over the fat round piers these ribs spring from stone brackets, or corbels, set into the wall. The other type of pier, however, carries its shaft right up to the clerestory level and the ribs spring from its capital, while at the same time a substantial transverse arch crosses the nave at right angles, dividing the vault visually into double rather than single bays. Especially intriguing is the fact that in order to raise these transverse arches to the same height as the diagonal ones, they have to be pointed, thus producing another crucial feature of the Gothic style. Yet the whole interior was complete by 1133, and must have been designed throughout by the first master of 1093.

The Normans, unlike most of the peoples of 11th-century Europe, had no fondness for figure sculpture, so that English cathedrals of this period are disappointingly bare compared with those of other countries. At Durham, however, they did make one irresistible concession to fantasy – the demon's head on the north door which holds the great sanctuary knocker in its mouth.

After 1133 Durham received only two major additions that were not part of the original plan. About 1170 a Lady Chapel, or Galilee, was built up against the west front, a highly unusual position for which no adequate explanation is forthcoming. Resembling the hall of a secular palace, it is a single-story building divided into three by arcades of highly decorated round arches. Then in 1242 the old east end (which had been apsidal, like Santiago) was pulled down, and a new straight east end was begun, crossing the chancel at right angles

and projecting like a transept. This is the Chapel of the Nine Altars. It was not finished until about 1280, by which time the first English Gothic style (Early English) was beginning to evolve into Decorated. It has all the slim elegance of the early style, carried perhaps even to excess (the ground level drops, and this allowed greater height without disturbing the roof-line), with clustered shafts of black Purbeck marble and beautifully logical bar tracery inherited from Lincoln (see p. 36).

Of later alterations the most serious were the insertion of large Decorated or Perpendicular windows into the east and west fronts and at the ends of the transepts. The east window was in its turn replaced in 1795 by James Wyatt's present rose window, unworthy of its setting. At the same time Wyatt had the idea – fortunately not carried out – of removing the Galilee altogether in order to make a drive for the bishop's carriage past the west front.

Durham. Interior looking east. Note the geometrical patterning of the round columns. The rose window is an 18th-century replacement.

Winchester

WINCHESTER was begun shortly before Durham, but later alterations have left it a Romanesque structure in only one part–the transepts. Here the primitive strength of early Norman architecture can be felt more authentically than anywhere else in England. Aisles go right around the transepts, but they are completely unadorned, with heavy, roughly cut masonry, thick mortar and crude cushion capitals to the shafts. The main ceiling is, and always was, of wood, much the commonest way of covering a large Romanesque church; but the aisles are vaulted in stone, some groined, others with coarse ribs. To visualize the Norman cathedral we have to imagine an apsidal choir of four bays and a nave of eleven, all in the same forthright style.

The 12th and 13th centuries were Winchester's golden age. One vivid reflection of it is the famous Winchester Bible in the cathedral library. Two others, now sadly mutilated, are the wall-paintings in the chapel of the Holy Sepulchre and the sculpture of Ecclesia (or perhaps Synagogue) in the choir, both of about 1230.

Then in 1345 Bishop Edington began a complete remodeling of the nave, carried on after his death in 1366 by William of Wykeham. It was done very economically, not by demolishing the old Norman work and rebuilding, but by careful subtraction, recarving and refacing of what was already there. First the gallery was removed altogether, thus reducing the elevation from three stories to two and nearly doubling the height of the arcade. The top part of this (corresponding with the arches of the old gallery) was covered with blank tracery and became a triforium. Above that the old clerestory was retained, with an enlarged window and more blank tracery linking it with the arcade underneath. The main Norman wall shafts were recarved and made to support a new stone vault (the old ceiling had been of wood). All this was in the new Perpendicular style that had arisen in the mid-14th century in reaction to the eccentricities of Decorated (e.g. the Ely octagon, pp. 20, 24, or Wells retrochoir, p. 31). Moldings are thin and shallow, straight lines are preferred to curves, repetition to variety. The actual structure is not outwardly expressed, as it had been in earlier Gothic styles, but is covered by a tight network of patterns that can be adapted to both window tracery and vaulting ribs.

Winchester's 14th-century nave is a remodeling of the 11th-century structure, but the intricate Perpendicular vault actually rests on the original Norman wall shafts.

Winchester. The north transept, the only part of the cathedral still in its original early Norman state.

Ely

NEARLY all medieval cathedrals are the result of slow growth, changes in style, alterations and additions, and for some reason this applies with more force in England than in any other country. We have seen it happening at Durham and at Winchester. In no case is the process more striking than at Ely. The present appearance, especially from a distance, is as magical as anything in Europe – yet no one architect ever meant it to look like that. It is the product of accumulated accidents. The original Norman cathedral must have looked something like Durham, except that instead of two west towers there was only one, with flanking bays forming a short western transept. Then in the mid-13th century the eastern apse was pulled down and replaced by a much larger Early English east end with lancet windows. In 1322 the central tower collapsed and was replaced by the octagon, a completely original design in the Decorated style. At the same time the Lady Chapel was added to the north transept. Later in the 14th century the west tower was given its octagonal top, and finally (or maybe not finally – nobody knows when it happened) the northern half of the west transept fell down and has been a ruin ever since. So everything about Ely has changed: the plan, the windows, above all the silhouette. Yet it remains an aesthetic unity, more fascinating in its coherent disharmony than most buildings that sprang complete from the brain of one designer.

Above *Detail from the interior of the Lady Chapel. Although the sculpture is mutilated, the "nodding ogee" canopy and the complicated play of interpenetrating shapes make it a masterpiece of the Decorated style.*

Left *Ely. The octagon from below. Built in the 1320s to replace the collapsed crossing tower, it is a most ambitious and original work of medieval carpentry.*

The west front of Ely is a mixture of different periods: tower and transept on the right are Norman, the porch in the center Early English and the octagonal top Perpendicular. The matching left-hand transept collapsed in medieval times.

To gain an idea of the Norman building, which was begun in 1083, we have to go to the nave and transepts. The nave looks very much as that of Winchester did before it was remodeled. It is very long–twelve bays (originally thirteen, as we shall see). The piers of the arcade are of two forms which alternate, though they are not so contrasted as at Durham, and all have shafts going without a break from floor to ceiling. The gallery, as usual, is subdivided into two, and the clerestory into three. The ceiling is of wood: what we see today is a Victorian imitation, but excellently done and no doubt close to the original. The big single west tower is unusual in England, though frequent enough in Germany (see p. 24). One precious relic of the Norman decoration is the Prior's Door, from the cloister into the nave, with its sculptured tympanum reminiscent of Burgundy.

Above *Ely. The Early English east end. The two shafts visible beyond the stalls mark the eastern end of the old Romanesque east end.*

Above left *The Prior's Door led from the cloister to the nave. The jambs are covered with foliage and circles enclosing a multitude of exotic figures, while in the tympanum sits Christ, his mandorla supported by two angels.*

Above right *Ely. The nave looking towards the octagon and the east end. The sturdy proportions, emphatic gallery and extreme length are typical of English Romanesque.*

By about 1200 the builders had reached the west front, and here the history of styles can be read almost as in a textbook. The lower four stages are richly ornamented Romanesque, a profusion of round arches and intricate geometrical patterns. The fifth uses the pointed arch and slightly less ornament; and the two corner octagons at the end of the south-western transept and the lower stages of the west tower continue in this style. The porch was begun in 1215 and is in the mature Early English of Salisbury or Lincoln.

Soon after the porch was finished the prior and chapter must have decided to rebuild the east end. Probably they took the normal course of building outside the apse wall until all was ready and they could simply demolish the apse and join the new work to the old. This new choir (1234–52) can best be understood by leaving Ely and looking forward to the nave

of Lincoln (p. 34), where the Early English style had just been worked out to its full perfection: slender piers surrounded by eight Purbeck shafts, stiff-leaf capitals, vaulting shafts resting on foliage corbels, a tierceron vault with its multiplication of ribs springing from a single point. The master of Ely developed all these features and passed them back to Lincoln, even more enriched, where they culminated, after 1252, in the Angel Choir.

Then on February 12, 1322, disaster. The central tower fell, bringing down with it all the old Norman choir, but leaving the later extension intact. The sacrist in charge of the rebuilding, Alan of Walsingham, must have been a man of unusual vision, and was able to call on an equally talented artist, William Hurley, the King's carpenter, to make it a reality. Instead of re-erecting the four piers which had supported the tower, they chose a completely new solution. By demolishing the four aisle bays at each corner they transformed the crossing from a square into an octagon. Four sides corresponded in height and width to the old crossing arches, though set back by one bay. The other four were lower *diagonal* arches cutting across the old corner bays. Above these diagonal arches they inserted huge windows with complicated curvilinear tracery, and for a vault built a wooden octagonal lantern which seems to be supported only on its own slender ribs, bringing yet more light into the center of the church. The structural skeleton is in fact behind all this, and consists of sixteen giant beams leaning inwards and meeting in a ring just beneath the lantern windows.

Ely octagon epitomizes that spirit of spatial boldness which is the essence of the Decorated style. But it did not exhaust the imagination of its builders. As soon as it was finished they set to work on the Lady Chapel (begun before the collapse), which abounds in yet more inventive play: large windows with odd, unexpected shapes in the tracery; rows of seats against the wall with ogee canopies (i.e. made up of two s-curves meeting at the top) which "nod" out in three dimensions; shafts which run behind the seats and *through* the canopies; a vault made up not merely of repeated tiercerons but of liernes as well, making the ceiling into a network of ribs.

Ely is indeed a pattern-book of English architecture from the late 11th to the mid-14th century. Yet no cathedral anywhere is more assertively and unmistakably itself.

Worms

LIKE all European countries, Germany had her own individual brand of Romanesque, and in fact remained faithful to it long after the others had succumbed to the novel charms of Gothic. Its most noticeable peculiarity – which can be traced back to the age of Charlemagne – is the so-called "westwork," a tower, or at least a tall structure, often with an apse, at the west end, balancing the choir and crossing at the east. A few English cathedrals, for instance Ely, experimented with this idea, but German Romanesque cathedrals take it much farther. Sometimes they actually look almost identical at both ends, with no obvious way in. A second characteristic is their fondness for pairs of tall narrow towers (really only staircase turrets) flanking nave, choir or transept and giving them a highly romantic silhouette.

Worms illustrates both these features. The basic fabric goes back to about the year 1000, easily recognizable in the nave arcade with its heavy square piers and primitive moldings. There is no gallery, only a bare expanse of wall between arcade and clerestory. In about 1170 it was decided to vault the church, and this was done by placing shafts against every other pier and building square vaults over the double bays, a crude enough arrangement when one compares it to contemporary work in France or England. Together with the building of the westwork, this took until about 1230.

The east and west ends, separated in date by about 200 years, are surprisingly similar. The earlier is in many ways the more interesting, with some endearingly ferocious lions growling on the exterior window sills. The west end, which is polygonal in plan, is adorned with four rose windows and – on the interior – two more circular depressions, all rather like cake patterns stamped out of pastry. The exterior shows another favorite motif of German Romanesque, the "dwarf galleries" formed by rows of colonnettes, which run across both east and west ends and around the central tower.

Left *The south side of Worms. The western apse, flanked by towers, is on the left. Near the middle is the crossing tower and transept, and on the right the east end, also flanked by towers.*

Right *Worms. The west end. This development of a western apse flanked by towers was a particular feature of German Romanesque.*

William of Sens' new choir of Canterbury, the first developed Gothic in England. Note the sexpartite vaulting, and at the far end the coupled columns derived from his native city.

*Canterbury from the south. From left to right:
the twin towers of the west front, the nave, the
crossing tower with main transepts, the choir, the*
*eastern crossing, the old apse, William of Sens'
eastern extension (Trinity Chapel) and finally
the "Corona" at the extreme east end.*

Canterbury

CANTERBURY has a special place in architectural history for three reasons. First, it is the mother church of England, the place where St. Augustine began his mission in 597. Secondly, it is the place where the French Gothic style was introduced into England in 1175. And thirdly, we possess in the monk Gervase's description of the burning and repair of Canterbury (*De Combustione et Reparatione Cantuariensis Ecclesiae*) the only detailed eyewitness account of the building of an early medieval cathedral.

The church which Gervase saw catch fire on September 5, 1174, was itself of two periods. A Norman cathedral on the conventional pattern had been built between 1070 and 1077 by the first Norman archbishop, Lanfranc: apsed choir, crossing, transepts, nave and west front with twin towers. Hardly was that finished than Lanfranc's successor, Anselm, pulled down the choir and extended the east end by a new choir, an extra pair of transepts and another apse, to which were attached three chapels, thus doubling the length of the church as a whole. This work was finished in 1130, and the exterior walls, as well as the crypt beneath it, survive virtually intact today. The plan is complex, the decoration lavish. Of stone carving the capitals of the crypt provided by far the liveliest examples, with fabulous animals fighting or playing musical instruments.

Capital in the crypt of Canterbury. A complex two-headed monster holds a fish and a pod with seven peas. What it means, no one knows.

This was the church–Lanfranc's nave and Anselm's choir–which saw the martyrdom of Thomas Becket in 1170. He had come from the bishop's palace on the other side of the cloister, entered the door of the north transept pursued by the four knights, and was murdered on a flight of steps approaching the side of the high altar. It was an event which at a worldly level had its compensations for Canterbury. Becket was immediately hailed as a saint, miracles began to occur at his tomb, and the cathedral was soon one of the richest in Europe.

Then in 1174 came the fire. It destroyed only the choir, leaving the nave untouched. "The brethren consulted," says Gervase, "how and by what method the ruined church might be repaired. Architects, both French and English, were therefore assembled, but they disagreed in their opinions. Some undertook to repair, while others, on the contrary, affirmed that the whole church must be taken down if the monks wished to dwell in safety. This, though true, overwhelmed them with grief. Among the architects was one, William of Sens, a man of great abilities and a most curious workman in wood and stone. Neglecting the rest, him they chose for the undertaking."

The choice was significant. The rebuilding of the cathedral of William's home town of Sens had begun in 1143, and the style was Gothic. Gothic was already taking root in England (Wells, as we shall see, owed little to French influence), but the Gothic used by William of Sens at Canterbury gave it a decisive new direction. It was an architecture of line rather than of volume, of forces held in equilibrium rather than of weight supported by mass. Where Romanesque buildings are massively strong, Gothic ones are slender, tense and elegant. In practical terms it meant doing away with load-bearing walls and transferring all the weight to piers and arches, and to do this the Gothic architect used three technical devices: the rib vault (which concentrates the weight of the vault on those points where the ribs spring from their piers), the pointed arch (which is stronger than the round arch but exerts a thrust outwards as well as downwards), and the flying buttress (really a half-arch counteracting the outward thrust by itself exerting an equivalent pressure in the opposite direction). Canterbury represents Gothic in process of evolution. Its source lies in the cathedrals of northern France built between 1145 and 1170. Its culmination (p. 42) was to come at Chartres in 1194.

William kept the shell of Anselm's choir and demolished everything inside it. In its place he built a new choir with tall, slender piers (alternately round and octagonal in section, and at the corners of the crossing surrounded by eight Purbeck marble shafts), gallery and clerestory, and a rib vault divided into six cells by an extra transverse arch cutting across the middle ("sexpartite"). The proportions, as we know from Gervase, are taller than those of the

old choir, which meant heightening the windows too; the capitals are French stiff-leaf; and the use of doubled columns in the Trinity Chapel at the extreme east end is taken verbatim from Sens. But certain features remain, or make their appearance, which are typically English, for instance the use of zig-zag ornament (a Romanesque cliché) and of Purbeck marble for subsidiary shafts.

In 1179 William of Sens fell from the scaffolding where he was supervising the building of the vault. "He came to the ground from the height of the crown of the upper arch, which is fifty feet. Being grievously bruised he was utterly unable to attend to the work . . . At length, finding no benefit from the skill and attention of his surgeons, he gave up the work, and, crossing the sea, went home to France."

His successor was another William, an Englishman. He completed the choir and Trinity Chapel, a space intended for the shrine of St Thomas Becket. To build it the end of Anselm's apse was removed together with its central chapel. At the very end of the church is the so-called *corona,* a small nearly circular chapel holding the *cathedra.*

The whole new choir was completed in 1184, just ten years after the fire. Becket's body was installed in its appropriately magnificent setting, and during the next thirty or forty years the windows were filled with stained glass, much of which survives. In the clerestory were large-scale figures of prophets, vivid images of great tragic power (many of these were later moved to the south-west transept); but the aisle windows, which could be examined close to, revealed tiny scenes in squares, roundels or lozenge shapes, telling stories of the miracles at St Thomas's shrine.

So Canterbury remained for 200 years, still with Lanfranc's early, and increasingly primitive-looking, Norman nave. In 1391 Henry Yevele, the King's master mason, was commissioned to rebuild it. He seems consciously to have followed the precedent of Winchester nave, though here demolishing and rebuilding, not remodeling. The two old towers were the last to go, one in 1424, the other not until 1832. Finally, in 1496, John Wastell designed the superb crossing tower, Bell Harry, which is today the dominant feature of the exterior and one of the great glories of Perpendicular architecture.

Wells chapter house, 14th century. Such octagonal chapter houses with a vault supported on a single pier were unique to England.

The great strainer arches, inserted in the 14th century into the 13th-century crossing of Wells to provide interior buttressing for the new tower.

Wells

WELLS, begun a few years after William of Sens started to rebuild Canterbury, enters architectural history twice. In its original form (about 1180–1240) it represents the emergence of a purely English type of Gothic, while the alterations and additions made between 1290 and 1340 are among the highlights of the Decorated style.

Of the original Wells only the transepts and the nave survive in easily recognizable form. The contrast with Canterbury is striking. At Canterbury, William had emphasized the dynamics of his architecture by, as it were, laying bare the skeleton; carrying the vaulting shafts down through the gallery and resting them on clearly defined supports. The Wells master seems concerned to do just the opposite. His piers are not single columns but complex clusters of shafts which conceal rather than display the line of thrust. Similarly, the gallery (actually a triforium, as it has nothing behind it) is not a series of arches with the line of stress going clearly between them, as at Canterbury, but an unbroken row which completely ignores the bay divisions of both arcade below and vault above. Finally, the proportions are kept low, the arches wide, the supports thick, leading the eye not upward to the vault but forward to the crossing. All these are qualities which we associate more with Romanesque than with Gothic, but which English architects clearly had no wish to forego. The same can be said of the Wells west front, which was reached towards the end of

Wells. The west front. The statuary in the niches constitutes the most complete survival in England of a medieval sculptural scheme.

the 12th century. Instead of expressing the structure behind and forming a ceremonial preparation for it, it is a screen for the display of figure sculpture. Above the level of the sculpture the master's intentions are unknown. Possibly he planned to have towers like the ones actually built 200 years later, possibly not.

In 1286 a whole series of new works was undertaken. It included the Chapter House, with its superb central pier fanning out into thirty-six ribs, the apotheosis of the tierceron vault; a remodeling of the chancel; and a new Lady Chapel at the extreme east end. It is where the elongated octagon of the Lady Chapel interpenetrates the rectangle of the retrochoir that the great visual complications occur. It is a space hard to illustrate and impossible to describe, but the ribs interlock in such a variety

of ways that at one point even so accomplished a master was left with two ribs and no capital to bring them down on—and solved the problem by producing a lion's head which obligingly bites them off short.

In about 1340 extra internal buttresses, the so-called strainer arches, were inserted under the crossing because the central tower proved too heavy for its supports. They were given the form of low pointed arches, coming right down to the floor without capitals, and carrying *inverted* arches on top of them. In the triangular spaces between the two arches are large roundels, like eyes above a gaping mouth.

One would dearly like to know the feelings of the man who designed the arches. Did he realize how brutally he was disturbing the quiet rhythms of his predecessor?

Lincoln

THE present Lincoln Cathedral was begun in 1192 and finished about 1280–that is, it represents the next phase of English Gothic after Canterbury. There had, however, been a Norman cathedral here, and of this one very substantial part remains: the west front, a symmetrical composition of five arches–one large, containing the principal doorway and a large window, two smaller ones corresponding to the aisles, and two flanking niches. Behind it, but curiously set back ten feet or so, were two square towers, which again survive, though heightened later. The whole composition thus combined the twin-towered façade (e.g. Durham) with the English "screen" façade (e.g. Wells or Salisbury), and even in its present form still does so. Across the whole front ran a band of relief sculpture with scenes from the Old and New Testaments, a feature unique in England and paralleled only in northern Italy.

The crossing tower of Lincoln – Early English below, Decorated above.

Lincoln. The Angel Choir. Typical of the mature Early English style are the eight-light east window, the tierceron vault with ridge-rib and the delicate foliage carving.*

Left *Two small figures on a 14th-century screen in a chapel in the south transept, beneath a Latin inscription: "Pray for the benefactors of this church." The heads are modern restorations.*

In 1186 the energetic Hugh of Avalon became bishop, and finding the cathedral dilapidated and partly in ruins, decided on a complete rebuilding. The name of Geoffrey de Noyers is found in the records as *fabricae constructor,* though this does not necessarily mean that he was the architect.

The new church kept the same cruciform outline and the same dimensions as the old, but as at Canterbury, the east end was enlarged and given its own (eastern) pair of transepts. Anyone who has seen William of Sens' choir at Canterbury will have no difficulty in recognizing the derivation of Geoffrey de Noyers' at Lincoln. The elevation is closely similar in general terms and in details, such as the round and octagonal piers surrounded by clustered shafts of Purbeck marble. But Geoffrey's mind was more inventive than William's, and it is a peculiarly spatial form of inventiveness.

Let us look more closely at four features in particular. First: the crossing of choir and eastern transepts. Here only one of Geoffrey's piers remains, but it is extraordinary. It is surrounded by shafts, but behind these shafts the core sprouts out in sprays of foliage. Second: the south-east transept end, which has what looks like an aisle supporting a two-story screen reaching to the roof. But this serves no purpose and is merely a false front through which one sees the real front beyond. Third: the blank arcade running around the aisle walls. This is normal enough in English architecture, and even the intersecting arcade, where one row of arches seems to overlap another, is not uncommon. But Geoffrey actually does place one arcade in front of the other, and to make sure that we do not miss this fact he leaves a hole in the spandrel of the one in front through which we see the apex of the one behind (most of these holes were later filled with sculptured heads). Fourth: the

vault, the "Crazy Vault" of Lincoln. We have seen quadripartite vaults at Durham and Wells, sexpartite at Canterbury (and here, in the eastern transept of Lincoln). But that of Lincoln choir is a sort of cross between the two, a pattern that is almost impossible to describe. First, there is a rib running all along the apex of the vault, the first ridge-rib in Europe. Then it looks somehow as if the diagonal ribs had set out to meet each other in the middle of each bay and missed, so that one gets two points of intersection with the ridge-rib instead of one. It is a strange, limping rhythm, but fits well with the quirky personality of its builder.

This first master (Geoffrey, if it was he) must have died early in the 13th century, when only the east end and part of the transept had been built. Later architects (of whom the most important was called Alexander) "reformed" Geoffrey, like schoolmasters correcting the work of a wayward student. The overlapping arcades became an orthodox single line. The vault was made regular in the main transepts by reviving the old sexpartite type, but in the nave a wholly new method was used – placing extra ribs of the same thickness on either side of the diagonal ones. In quadripartite and sexpartite vaults there is *one* point in each bay where the ribs meet the crown of the vault; in the Crazy Vault *two*; in the nave *three*. The result is that the division into bays is no longer easily seen, and instead one is conscious of the bunches of ribs sprouting out from the wall shafts, seven on each side. It is the beginning of an English speciality, the tierceron vault.

One of the angels in the spandrels of the gallery of the Angel Choir. He is weighing souls, holding the balance (much damaged) in his left hand. The saved rest in his lap; the damned fall headlong to hell.

By about 1235 the new work had reached the old Norman west front, and instead of demolishing it (as a French architect would almost certainly have done) the English master built around it, leaving it embedded in his extended screen of interlaced arcades and multiplicity of shafts.

The nave and transepts of Lincoln represent the culmination of the lancet style, i.e. the first phase of Early English before the coming of bar tracery. All the original windows are lancets, except the rose window of the north transept, the Dean's Eye, which is composed of circles and trefoils. But fairly soon after this was completed Geoffrey's east end was taken down (it is the familiar story again) and the cathedral lengthened to the east by a new choir, the Angel Choir. The elements of the design are those of the nave, but with even more enrichment. The corbels supporting the vaulting shafts are now immense bunches of foliage, while in the spandrels of the gallery sit the music-playing angels that give the choir its name. For the first time at Lincoln, too, bar tracery is used (it had originated in France some forty years before—see p. 43), culminating in the splendid east window of eight lights crowned by graduated circles.

The Decorated style touched Lincoln only once, in the 1330s, when the south transept rose window, the Bishop's Eye, corresponding to the Dean's Eye opposite, was replaced by a composition of sinuous flowing tracery. The contrast between Early English logic and Decorated freedom could not be more neatly demonstrated.

Salisbury

AS Durham is a copybook Romanesque cathedral, Salisbury–to an even greater degree–is copybook Early English. It was designed for an unoccupied site, built except for the spire in a single campaign, and has entirely escaped structural alteration.

The town, castle and cathedral of Salisbury were originally at Old Sarum, $1\frac{1}{4}$ miles away, "exposed to the wind, barren, dry and isolated," as one of its canons wrote. In 1219 Bishop Poore was given papal permission to build a new cathedral in the valley. It was begun in the following year, 1220, and finished about 1266. Salisbury thus has a consistency of style that makes it unique in England.

Left *Salisbury from the south-west. English Gothic, in contrast to French, favored screen west fronts, the main ceremonial entrance being by a porch on one side.*

Right *Salisbury. Interior looking east. Salisbury's appearance is due partly to its very restrained Early English style, partly to the loss of its chapels and screens in the 18th century.*

Below *Salisbury. The chapter house. Above the blank arcade at seat level runs a series of scenes, now largely destroyed, carved in relief and telling the story of the Creation.*

First the plan. We have seen how the idea of double transepts, which had originated almost accidentally at Canterbury, had been taken up at Lincoln. Salisbury follows closely. As at Lincoln, the smaller (eastern) transepts project two bays, the main (western) ones three. As at Lincoln also, both transepts are without aisles but have chapels along their eastern sides. Even more than at Lincoln, one feels that the master mason saw his cathedral as an assembly of distinct rectilinear parts, an effect specially noticeable in the view from the east, where the Lady Chapel, retrochoir, choir aisles, transept chapels, choir and crossing rise in a series of clear steps to culminate in the central tower. In a contemporary French cathedral all these elements would be drawn together to form a tight unity of mass (Rheims, Amiens or Bourges); in England, slightly later, they would merge into and through each other in a way that baffles and intrigues the eye.

One gets the same impression from the details of the interior. Even more than at Wells, the emphasis is upon horizontals rather than verticals—a clear separation of arcade, gallery and clerestory levels. The nave arcade consists of circular columns with four attached shafts, each one visibly separate from the column, not (as at Wells) clustering closely to it. The use of black Purbeck marble for the nave arcade and the shafts of the gallery makes each part even more distinct. This Purbeck marble is the only touch of luxury that the Salisbury master allows himself: no tracery, only lancet windows; virtually no naturalistic carving, only severe rounded moldings; no stained glass, only monochrome grisaille (now mostly replaced). The severity of Salisbury has been exaggerated by Wyatt's demolition of chantries and screens in the 18th century, but it was present from the beginning.

The west front problem continued to give trouble to English architects. That of Salisbury, like Wells, is a screen, overlapping and concealing the elevation behind, and providing a setting for the display of figure sculpture, of which none now remains. But the doorways are pathetically insignificant for such a building.

In 1334 the central crossing tower was heightened and crowned by the tallest spire in the world. Contrary though it was to the first master's intention, no purist has ever been pure enough to regret it.

Right The famous and fabulous beasts on the towers of Notre Dame are the fruits of the careful restoration by Viollet-le-Duc.

Notre Dame, Paris

THE Gothic style was evolving in the Ile de France, the region around Paris, between 1140 and 1190, and we have seen the spin-off from events there affecting English cathedrals from the later 12th century onwards. In architecture it meant essentially the combination of the pointed arch, the rib vault and the flying buttress to convey not only aesthetic excitement but also a tense, balanced harmony of forces symbolic of spiritual aspiration. In sculpture it meant a new naturalism, a new freedom of gesture and expression; in painting and stained glass a similar transformation—a gain in elegance without any slackening of emotive power.

To trace the evolution of the new style in its homeland we must go back in time a little and look at a building which represents its earliest phase, already clearly distinct from Romanesque but not yet fully aware of the potentialities of Gothic. The foundation stone of Notre Dame was laid in 1163. From its plan alone we can deduce a new era: instead of being compartmented and spread out, visually divisible into its parts (as French Romanesque had been and English Gothic continued to be), Paris is compact and unified. Transepts there are, but they were originally only two bays long and so did not project beyond the double aisles of nave and choir. Nor were there, in the original scheme, any attached chapels; when these were added in the 13th century, they were accommodated, unobtrusively, between the buttresses. And from an engineering point of view Notre Dame led Europe: it seems certain that it was during the course of building (some time after 1180) that flying buttresses were deliberately exposed to view, the recognized components of a new style.

Above *Notre Dame. The west front. French Gothic cathedrals almost invariably used a monumental two-towered design expressing the structure of the interior. After Notre Dame this basic design was to be developed in an increasingly dramatic way.*

Right *The tympanum of the north transept (c. 1250), dedicated to the Virgin. The upper divisions relate the story of the cleric Theophilus, while those below show scenes from the infancy of Christ.*

Left *Notre Dame. Interior looking west down the nave from the crossing. On the right can be seen two of the bays restored in the mid-19th century to their original four-story elevation.*

Right *Notre Dame seen from the river Seine. The spire, flying buttresses and pierced stonework are of the High Gothic style, imposed on the main Early Gothic structure at a later date.*

In numberless ways, therefore, Notre Dame looks forward to the great age of Gothic architecture that was shortly to come. But just because it was so soon to be surpassed by Chartres, Rheims, and Amiens, it is very hard not to see it as a series of slightly missed chances. The interior elevation, for instance, has a clearly intended vertical emphasis. Higher and narrower than any English cathedral, its clusters of triple shafts carry the lines of the vault downwards—but only to the capitals of the arcade. The master did not yet think of his whole interior as a complete skeleton of ribs. The arcade piers themselves are thick, sturdy and short—earthbound, not soaring. Upon them rests a gallery that is as tall and almost as substantial as the arcade, again denying the vertical movement. Above the gallery is the clerestory, which in the original design was divided into two levels—first a round window with a wheel pattern, punched into the wall as we have seen it in Romanesque Germany, and above that a large single light. Soon after they were built, perhaps when the system of flying buttresses was introduced, these were replaced by a more unified arrangement of simple plate tracery, two lancets crowned by a circle. Viollet-le-Duc in the 19th century restored a few bays near the crossing to their earlier appearance.

All this suggests a certain irresolution on the part of the master mason, a fumbling for a logic which was somehow beyond his grasp. The vault—to follow through this analysis—is sexpartite, a system which to be consistent demands alternation of supports such as we have seen, for instance, at Durham: main ones for the transverse arches, minor ones for the subsidiary ribs. At Notre Dame the master made all his supports identical, even placing sets of three wall shafts under every springing, though logic requires alternately three and five. But in the piers between the inner and outer aisles he seems to have been uneasily aware of the need to express the structure he had chosen, and did indeed provide alternating supports, a cluster of twelve thin shafts interposing themselves between the thick circular piers. And at the very west end, the last part to be built, he (or more probably his successor) publicly admitted one of his errors by bringing the wall shafts right down to the ground, though so inelegantly that one is tempted to wish that he had left well alone.

By 1235 Notre Dame was finished, very much as we know it, the last part being the west front with its towers. Compare this west front with any English example and the typical qualities of French Gothic are at once apparent: coherence, assurance, a clear expression of the fact that this is the ceremonial point of entry. The Notre Dame façade divides vertically into three, reflecting the internal divisions into nave and aisles (though not the fact that

there are double aisles). Crossing the three verticals are three main horizontals, at the level of the portals, of the rose window and of the screen of tracery at the top. Between the first and second comes a narrow band of statues, the so-called *Galerie des Rois*. Upon this solid and satisfying square rest the two towers, roughly half the height of the square. It is a proportion that expresses rest, not movement; flat pattern, not depth; Gothic in its forms but not yet truly Gothic in its spirit. Final judgment, however, must be suspended, since evidence has recently been produced that the whole front was colored.

The contrast between this façade of Notre Dame and those of Amiens and Rheims will be brought out in later chapters, but may be anticipated here by walking around to the north or south transept fronts. In about 1260 these were rebuilt and lengthened by Jean de Chelles with all the *panache* of mature Gothic: rose windows of sixteen lights blossoming in

their outer rings of thirty-two, and set in square frames which are themselves glazed, while beneath them spiky forms of gables and pinnacles cut through the horizontal lines, leading the eye relentlessly upward.

Notre Dame has suffered much from iconoclasts and restorers. Even before the Revolution it had lost its medieval glass, most of its tombs and some of its sculpture. After 1789 it was deprived of its treasure, and in the 19th century it underwent a restoration at the hands of Viollet-le-Duc which was drastic by any standards, though carried out with knowledge and imagination. Some of the most conspicuous and famous sculpture on the cathedral, such as the gargoyles on the towers, dates from this period, though much of first-class quality remains on the west front and the transept portals, and the foliage carving is superb throughout. The subject of Gothic sculpture, however, will have to be deferred until the next chapter.

Below *The Portail Royal at Chartres, the earliest surviving example (c. 1145) of a Gothic figured portal, and* (bottom), *a detail of the sculpture. Note the elongated proportions, stiff incised drapery patterns and feet pointing downwards.*

Chartres

W HAT had been tentatively sketched at Paris was fully and triumphantly realized at Chartres. Chartres stands at a crucial point in architectural history, the "classic moment" when Gothic reached its maturity, with all the elements finally resolved that were to dominate French architecture (and to a lesser extent English, Spanish and German) for centuries to come. But Chartres does not mean architecture only. It also possesses a profusion of sculpture produced by some of the greatest masters of that or any other time. And, as if that were not enough, the whole of its 13th-century stained glass survives complete. If the whole achievement of medieval art had to be represented by a single work, Chartres cathedral would be the only possible choice.

Building began in 1194 after a fire had almost completely destroyed the previous cathedral. Architecturally it is easy to grasp. French Gothic had none of that hankering after mystery that crops up so often in England. It has the usual cruciform plan, the transepts projecting only two bays and the east end consisting of an apse with a double aisle and radiating chapels. The arcade piers have only four shafts, one in each of the main directions,

Chartres. The interior looking east. The classic French Gothic solution is here fully realized for the first time – tall arcade and clerestory, with a less emphatic gallery; shafts running from floor to vault; quadripartite vault.

the inner one continuing straight up into the vault where it becomes the transverse arch defining the bay. The vault is orthodox quadripartite, without a ridge-rib. There are the usual clerestory and gallery, the latter reduced in importance so that it in no way competes, as it does at Notre Dame, with the arcade below or the clerestory above. The whole emphasis is vertical, the eye being led naturally up to the crown of the vault. The clerestory windows are divided into two large lights, too large to be called lancets, above which a miniature rose window is, as it were, punched into the masonry. This is "plate tracery," a short-lived preliminary stage before bar tracery was invented.

On the exterior the structural system is made explicit by flying buttresses, originally heavy in design, later strengthened by more elegant half-arches, expressing that same upward movement for which the Chartres master was striving in the ribs and shafts of the interior. He planned to go further still. Chartres was to be ringed by towers and spires – two at the west end, one over the crossing, two flanking each transept, two flanking the choir: nine altogether. Of these only two were actually built – those of the west front – and only one in the form he intended. But the substructure of the others can clearly be seen, reaching as far as roof level.

To many people all medieval sculpture looks much the same. Chartres is an excellent place to learn how false that is. Merely by walking around the building one can see with one's own eyes the very striking changes that took place in the crucial hundred years between 1140 and 1240. The oldest figures are in fact older than the cathedral we have been describing. All the west front between the towers, as far as the rose window, belongs to its predecessor and dates from about 1145. It consists of three portals, flanked by full-length figures representing kings and patriarchs from the Old Testament. Their drapery falls in stiff, shallow folds, their toes point downwards as if they were without weight, their arms are pressed close to their sides, their bodies are thin and elongated, still barely separate from the shafts against which they stand. Their faces, with strange, high cheek-bones, stylized hair and beards and remote, withdrawn expressions, seem those of spiritual messengers rather than ordinary human beings. These are among the first masterpieces of Gothic sculpture, still Romanesque in their hieratic stillness, but beginning to breathe with a new life.

Chartres. The west front. This is a complicated part of the cathedral, involving several changes of plan; the lower part of the center and the two towers date from about 1145, the rose window and the right-hand spire from about 1200, and the left-hand spire from 1507–13.

About 1220 it was decided to give equally grand portals to the north and south transepts. The arrangement is roughly the same as that of the west front (and, as we shall see, as that of Rheims and Amiens and numberless other large churches). But the figures belong to a new race, shorter in their proportions, more varied in their poses, more natural and relaxed in their gestures. The drapery still consists of long repeated folds, but it is now more deeply modeled, revealing the body beneath. Though still placed against the shafts of the portal, they are no longer half architectural but wholly sculptural.

Ten years or so later, in the 1230s, these portals were turned into porches by extending them and roofing them with gables. New figures were added, now carved with the full maturity of Gothic naturalism. In easy, noble stances, they rest their full weight on the pedestal that supports them. Their clothing is as varied as real material, some flat, some pulled into a hundred tiny folds, some heavy, sweeping down the body in a single graceful movement. Their heads are as realistic as portraits, but subtly intensified to convey a radiant, ideal beauty.

Below *Detail from Chartres' unrivaled wealth of 13th-century stained glass. The scenes (starting bottom left) include the Annunciation, Visitation, Nativity and the Adoration of the Magi.*

Bottom *Later sculpture from the north porch. The three figures on the left (c. 1220) still have some of the stylization of the earlier work, while that on the right (c. 1230) is naturalistic.*

Chartres' stained glass needs a book in itself. What impresses one at first is the sheer quantity. One is surrounded by it from the aisle windows almost to the height of the vault. Its colors are so rich that the sunlight is shut out and the actual building can be seen only dimly amid colored shadows. At ground level each window is made up of twenty or thirty small pictorial panels telling stories from the Old and New Testaments, legends or lives of the saints. Above, in the clerestory, where such details would be invisible, each window contains a single giant figure: dark faces, glowing eyes, and clothes shining like Aaron's breastplate. Chartres is indeed a whole collection of experiences, which no number of visits can come near to exhausting.

45

Rheims

OUR next four cathedrals are all French and are all close to Chartres in time and place. Bourges lies to the south, Rheims, Amiens and Beauvais to the north-east. Bourges was begun in 1192, Rheims in 1210, Amiens in 1220, and Beauvais in 1248. Though each has its own very strong personality, all belong to the same school, with the same ideals, which can be summarized as the urge to ever greater height and ever greater lightness.

Above *Rheims. The west front. Compare this with the west front of Notre Dame, Paris (page 39) to see how, between the early and the late 13th century, the surface has been given depth and the lines charged with energy.*

Right *The east end of Rheims is a milestone in architectural history, for it was here, about 1210, that bar tracery seems to have been invented. Between the chapels, heavy pinnacles provide abutments for the two tiers of flying buttresses.*

The old cathedral of Rheims, coronation place of the kings of France, was destroyed by fire in 1210. Rebuilding began at once, as usual at the east end, and proceeded quickly. By about 1250 the west front was started, though the higher parts were left unfinished until much later. The plan is essentially the same as that of Chartres, but in accordance with a general tendency among French buildings towards unity of space and volume, the transepts now project only one bay. The interior elevation also follows Chartres very closely, with the same four shafts attached to the arcade piers, the same fairly low gallery, the same tall clerestory windows divided into two lights, the same quadripartite rib vault. There was one very striking novelty about Rheims, however, and that appeared at the very beginning of its building history, in the windows of the ambulatory chapels – bar tracery.

Bar tracery meant a revolution in the way windows were seen in relation to walls. Designers no longer thought of the separate lights of a window as holes separated by masonry, but of the whole window as one unity articulated by a linear pattern. At first, as at Rheims, this merely meant the marriage of two lancets and the circular window above them. Then it became clear that one could combine four or even eight lights, making a

correspondingly complicated pattern of circles at the top. The whole system neatly paralleled the development of shafts and ribs in the interior: now not only the walls and vault could be expressed in linear terms, but the windows too. We have already seen the results of this invention in England, in the east window of the Angel Choir at Lincoln (p. 36).

This east end of Rheims also marks the coming of age of the flying buttress. All around the apse these graceful half-arches of stone lean against the walls of the choir. They are in two tiers, taking two jumps, as it were, to reach the wall, and are crowned by monumental canopies containing statues (these add weight, so are not entirely ornamental).

At the opposite end of the cathedral, the west front must have been begun in the 1240s. Although work went on here for over forty years and it was eventually left unfinished in 1290 (pyramidal spires were originally intended), it remains incomparably the finest façade of this whole group. The effect of dynamic upward thrust is achieved by the use of pointed shapes which at every level penetrate the horizontal divisions of the architecture. Note, for instance, how the gables of the three portals penetrate the horizontal line beneath the rose window, while the tops of the four buttress canopies similarly penetrate the next level (two of these were destroyed in World War I). Above that, the bases of the

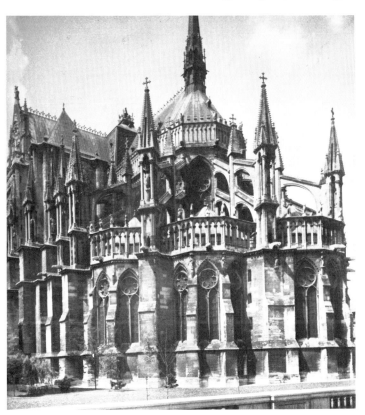

47

two towers are hidden behind a row of spiky forms, the gables of the *Galerie des Rois*. The towers themselves turn into octagons, with pointed angle turrets at the corners, and the whole design would no doubt have reached its climax in the spires. Whenever possible, too, the builders elongated the forms to stress their verticality, and made them transparent to emphasize lightness. The three tympana above the doors, which at Chartres and previous cathedrals had been filled with relief sculpture, are now glazed; the rose window itself is set, amazingly, within a framework of glass; while the tall openings into the towers on either side of it are not even glazed, but are left completely transparent, allowing views through to the flying buttresses of the nave.

Finally sculpture adds its contribution. In the gables of the three west portals (expelled, one might say, from the tympana) are scenes of the Crucifixion, the Coronation of the Virgin and Christ as Judge, each with a lively composition rising towards the center, though now mostly ruined by time and war. At the level of the rose window, each under his tall canopy, stand over-life-size figures of kings—probably Old Testament kings, though popularly identified with medieval kings of France. More kings appear in the *Galerie des Rois* at the top, the central ones participating in the baptism of Clovis, the first French Christian king. Over the rose window are (or were: these too are much damaged) reliefs of David and Goliath, the latter truly a giant, over 20 feet high.

Rheims is as rich and varied in its sculpture as Chartres, but it is more difficult to sort out chronologically, partly because several artists seem to have been working in different styles at more or less the same time, and partly because some of it seems to have been moved from the positions it originally occupied. It is nonetheless worth close study. That of the west front is particularly rewarding, especially the central portal. On one side four figures form a tableau of the Presentation in the Temple: the Virgin and St Simeon in the center, Joseph and a maidservant at the side. These latter two are in the style of the last phase of Chartres, relaxed, smiling and alert, aware of each other's presence. On the other side of the door stand two pairs—the Annunciation (the angel with the famous "Rheims smile") and the Visitation. These four illustrate the divergent styles being produced at Rheims simultaneously. The angel is in the style of the St. Joseph opposite; Mary in another, less assured manner which we shall meet again at

Above *Rheims, looking west from the roof of the south transept. At the bottom is the upper part of the flying buttresses. The towers were originally planned to finish with spires.*

Top *Sculpture on Rheims west front: the Annunciation (the angel with the famous "sourire de Rheims") and the Visitation.*

Right *Rheims. The nave looking west. Elevation and vaulting are essentially the same as at Chartres.*

48

Amiens; while the group of the Visitation is completely different, reminding one if anything of late classical sculpture, with its bunchy, deeply folded drapery and poses like those of a Roman matron. Several figures on the portals of the north transept are in this same Roman style, indicating that sculptors were looking at the remains of classical art which at that time were more plentiful than they are now.

Some of the most intriguing works of sculpture at Rheims are in places where one would not normally look. The whole inner west wall, for instance, below the level of the rose window, is carved into a series of trefoil-headed niches containing figures of kings, patriarchs and saints. Most amazing of all, and the least accessible, are some figures and heads high up on the exterior of the choir. Here the sculptor evidently felt free to indulge his fancies without reference to decorum, and the result is a strange mixture of grim realism and grotesque imagination.

Amiens

AMIENS was begun in 1220. Contrary to normal practice, the nave was built first (by 1236) and the east parts later (finished in 1269). The plan that we have seen evolving at Chartres and Rheims is in all essentials used again at Amiens: that is, nave with aisles, transepts, choir with double aisles and an apsidal ambulatory with chapels. Interior elevation and vaulting are modeled on Rheims, though the tendency towards unity and verticality is carried further: the transepts hardly project at all, and the proportion of height to width is greater, the tall piers of the arcade especially making an effect of superb grandeur, with (as at Chartres and Rheims) the main vaulting shafts carried uninterruptedly to the ground. Bar tracery appears throughout, with large four-light windows in the clerestory. In the east end the last part to be built – the middle story ceases to be an unlit gallery and is given windows of its own, thus admitting more light and increasing the feeling of slenderness in the architectural members.

The west front marks an intermediate stage between Chartres and Rheims. It is still put together basically from a series of horizontal layers: the three portals, an open gallery, a *Galerie des Rois*, and the rose window. But already the gables of the portals thrust through one horizontal, and the turrets of the buttresses another. In its use of depth, variety of motifs and interplay of shadows, the façade of Amiens is fully as interesting as Rheims. The two towers were of course intended to be identical, but were not finished until much later, the south one in the 14th century, the north in the 15th. Over the crossing is merely a slender spire of wood (the present one dates from 1527). The only other structural changes have been the building of chapels between the buttresses of the nave and the insertion of new tracery into all three of the rose windows. They date from the 14th century onwards, and are evidence of the influence of the Decorated style from England. For two centuries the pure logical style of Rheims resisted all fundamental changes; then about 1400 came *flamboyant*, and the tracery of rose windows flickered with shapes like flames or seemed to open like the petals of a flower. The sculpture of the west portals – "the Bible of Amiens," as Ruskin called it—is another vast subject which we can barely glance at. The large figures of apostles and prophets show a consistent style which corresponds roughly with the transept portals of Chartres and with a few groups (e.g. the Annunciation) at Rheims. Beneath them (a feature that does not occur elsewhere) is a double row of quatrefoils containing reliefs of scenes from the Bible, signs of the Zodiac and occupations of the months. These are among the freshest and most vivid of all medieval sculpture. The south transept has a portal of the same date, but with a central figure belonging to the 14th century, the famous *Vierge dorée*, epitome of late Gothic gaiety, sophistication and charm.

Something, indeed, of spiritual intensity disappeared from sculpture after 1300, but to see what it could still achieve even 200 years after that we have only to go inside and look at the wooden choir stalls. These were carved between 1508 and 1521, and consist of 110 seats arranged in two rows. From a distance all seems normal enough, but as one draws near one realizes that every available surface is alive with little figures enacting Biblical stories. On the stall-ends and misericords the scenes are in relief, but on the top they emerge into three dimensions, while still miraculously keeping the form and pattern of furniture.

Detail from the early 16th-century choir stalls of Amiens. At the top Pharaoh is represented twice— first dreaming of the fat kine, then of the lean. The reliefs below show the Presentation of the Virgin, and St. Anne teaching the Virgin to read.

Left *Amiens from the west. This photograph, taken before 1914, gives some idea of how the medieval cathedrals must have dominated the cities that huddled round them.*

Above *Amiens is in many ways the classic French Gothic cathedral, with its perfectly logical system of shafts, ribs and tracery and its carefully restrained ornament.*

Detail of 13th-century stained glass window at Bourges. St. Michael weighs souls; the devil tries to tip the balance.

Bourges

CHARTRES, Rheims and Amiens represent the classic perfection of French Gothic. Bourges, begun earlier (1192) but finished later than they were, is an eccentric, the work of a man who wanted to do something different.

First the plan. There are double aisles throughout, and no transept at all, so no distinction between nave and choir. The master mason obviously wanted a single, unified space leading without a break from one end to the other. He also wanted height, and he uses his double aisles in a way that had no precedent and had only one imitator (Le Mans). It can best be understood by imagining the normal interior elevation of a big Gothic church: arcade, gallery, clerestory. This elevation is used at Bourges (and Le Mans) for the *inner* aisle – that is, standing in the aisle and looking towards the outside of the church one would imagine oneself in the main space of an ordinary church looking towards the aisle. But if one then steps back into the nave at Bourges one sees the whole system repeated above: another gallery and another clerestory. This nave arcade, therefore, has to be immensely tall and the proportions of the three elements of the elevation are totally different from anything that had been used before.

The effect was certainly deliberate. Not content with bringing his shafts down from vault to floor, as was normal, the Bourges master makes the upper part of the wall itself bulge above the piers, as if the pier, in some hidden way, continued to rise above its capital. The vault, however, is a surprise, for it is sexpartite, a technique that Chartres had abandoned, and which fails to give the verticality of the piers its true consummation. The windows, too, have only old-fashioned plate tracery.

Bourges' west front was never carried through as intended. Logically, since the building had double aisles, there are five portals instead of the usual three, and twin towers were built over the two outer bays. Both, however, had faulty foundations. That on the south had to be buttressed by an inelegant leaning arch; that on the north collapsed in 1505 and was rebuilt on a larger scale. The total design fails to form a unity.

The sculpture, too, though of high quality, cannot be appreciated as an ensemble. The 13th-century portals have lost almost all their large figures. The reliefs in the tympana, however, survive, and the central one, of the Last Judgment, is among the most dramatic treatments of this subject in medieval art.

But if Bourges has been unlucky in many ways, it has been supremely lucky in its stained glass. Not only does the whole eastern part and its chapels retain its 13th-century windows – work on a level with those of Chartres and probably partly by the same artists – but there is also a wealth of later glass up to the 15th and 16th centuries.

Left *Bourges: the central portal of the west front. In the tympanum Christ sits as Judge, and beneath him St. Michael weighs souls.*

Below *Bourges looking east. It is the only great Gothic cathedral without a transept, so that the movement from west to east is uninterrupted.*

Below *Beauvais from the north. On the left is the choir, begun in 1248; in the center the* flamboyant *north transept by Martin Chambiges (1500 onwards).*

Bottom *The unfinished cathedral of Beauvais, from the air—choir and transepts but no nave. To the left of the transept can just be seen part of the ancient Carolingian cathedral which it was to replace.*

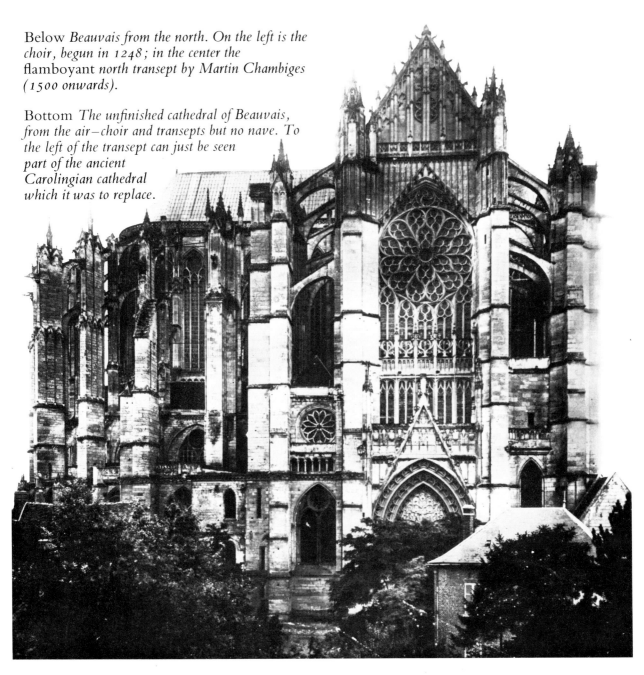

Beauvais

THE architects who designed the great Gothic cathedrals of France were building to the very limit of their engineering knowledge. Their mathematics was surprisingly sophisticated, but the science of statics hardly existed and no one could tell for certain how high one could build until one tried, and it either stood up or fell down. The nave of Notre Dame at Paris is 102 feet high; of Chartres 120 feet; of Bourges 122; of Rheims 124; of Amiens 140. At Beauvais they tried for 157 feet. The limit had been reached. The cathedral stands today unfinished, patched and more than slightly forlorn, but a monument to ambition and to professional daring.

The cathedral was begun in 1248. By the 1280s the whole choir was finished and the glass of the windows was being installed. The

The choir of Beauvais, looking east. It is hard in photographs to convey the sense of height, narrowness and light.

massive enough to resist the thrust directed at them. In 1284 they began to shift; the arcade and wall were pushed outwards and the vault collapsed, bringing down with it part of the clerestory and shattering the glass.

The damage was repaired immediately, but the master mason no longer dared to trust to the same system of supports. The number of piers in the arcade was doubled by inserting a new one between each pair of existing piers. The triforium was also strengthened and each clerestory window divided into two. The vault was changed from quadripartite to sexpartite, with transverse ribs carried on the new subsidiary piers. The result was a more stable but a less elegant design, the arcade especially looking uncomfortably cramped, with acutely pointed arches.

Although the choir in its revised form was finished and consecrated in 1322, further work did not resume until 1500. In that year the chapter of Beauvais commissioned Martin Chambiges of Paris, the leading architect of his age, to design the transepts and crossing, and these parts were built between then and 1550. In the interior Chambiges necessarily followed the earlier design closely, but when it came to the exterior, he felt free to assert the style of his own time, and the north and south transept fronts are exuberant exercises in mature *flamboyant*. Portals, buttresses and gables are covered with frilly ornaments of the most delicate kind, while the two identical rose windows hold an endless interlace of double-curving tracery (the southern one retains its glass of 1551).

It was still intended to complete the nave, but in the meantime (to show that the Beauvais spirit of tempting providence was not dead) the chapter decided to build a spire over the crossing taller than any spire in the world. Designed by Jean Vast it was in four stages, the first square (and open by windows to the crossing), the other three octagonal. The lowest three were of stone, the uppermost (91 feet) of wood, and the cross which crowned it was a proud 501 feet above the ground (Salisbury spire is a mere 404).

But again pride was running before a fall, and this time the fall was even swifter. The tower collapsed spectacularly on April 30, 1573, destroying much of the north transept as it fell. That damage too was heroically made good, but the tower was never rebuilt and the nave never begun. The Reformation and the Wars of Religion were already killing the spirit that built cathedrals.

plan belonged firmly in the mainstream of Rheims and Amiens: three bays with double aisles and an apse with seven radiating chapels. The elevation was also orthodox: tall arcade piers with shafts, a glazed triforium (as at Amiens) and tall clerestory windows with bar tracery; the vault, as one would expect, quadripartite. The only exceptional feature was the great height of all these elements. The piers, pared down to an extreme slenderness and standing over 30 feet apart, rose for 50 feet before they had any support at all from the vault of the aisle. Above that, the combined triforium and clerestory rose for another 50 feet without any abutment until the very top. The builders were certainly aware of the risks they were running, and tried to ensure safety by constructing flying buttresses of unprecedented height and with double rows of half-arches. But these buttresses were not

Below *Cologne Cathedral seen from the Rhine.
Begun in the 13th century, the building was not
completed till the 19th.*

Bottom *Cologne Cathedral in the 18th century,
with only the choir, part of the south-west
tower and the lower walls of the nave built.*

Cologne

THE story of Cologne cathedral in many
ways parallels that of Beauvais, but with
a happy ending. Like Beauvais, it was begun
to a vastly ambitious design in the mid-13th
century. Like Beauvais, work was broken off
when it had reached the crossing. Like Beauvais, it stood for 500 years, a giant, gaunt
fragment, looming over its city like a silent
reproach. The fact that work was taken up
again and triumphantly completed in the
middle of the 19th century was due to two
things: the discovery of the original medieval
designs (some in Darmstadt in 1812, others in
Paris in 1814) and an upsurge of collective
patriotism which made the finishing of the
cathedral in the "Germanic" style a symbol of
national achievement.

This cherishing of Cologne because of its Germanness is in fact somewhat ironic, since the original 13th-century building is to all intents and purposes a French cathedral on German soil. It is the logical successor of Amiens and Beauvais and, apart from its west front, would look far more at home in Picardy than in the Rhineland. The choir, with double aisles, ends in an apse with seven radiating chapels. The transepts project two bays (one bay more than Amiens or Beauvais). The nave (unlike Amiens, but probably like Beauvais as originally planned) is also double-aisled, but the aisles are of equal height and not stepped in the idiosyncratic style of Bourges. The nave is short by French standards—only five bays (Amiens has seven, Beauvais would have had six) but elevation and vaulting are again thoroughly French, with glazed triforium, large four-light clerestory windows and quad-ripartite vault. In height Cologne very nearly equals Beauvais (150 feet as against 157). In some respects, indeed, it goes further in emphasizing the vertical, since not only the main shafts carrying the transverse ribs but also the subsidiary ones carrying the diagonals are taken right down to the ground. On the other hand the placing of statues half way up the piers interrupts the verticals and has no parallel in France.

The choir was finished in 1322. Thereafter work proceeded slowly and intermittently. By 1388 the south transept was partially built, though only its eastern wall stood to its full height, and the nave had progressed as far as the level of the gallery. Then for some reason work was started on the façade, and the south tower was carried up to a considerable height. But in the 15th century very little was done, and in 1560 it was abandoned altogether. The great bulk of the choir, with the truncated tower a little distance from it, crowned by a tall crane, is a familiar sight in paintings and drawings.

Then in 1812 and 1814 the designs for the west front came to light. They are minutely detailed and reflect several changes of design, spreading over a period of possibly fifty years (about 1320 to 1370), though the essence remained the same. The problem, as at Bourges, was to create a façade that was a logical conclusion to a double-aisled interior. As at Bourges, the Cologne master expressed this by five divisions (originally five doors; later the two outer ones became windows), but now, instead of placing his towers over the outer aisle only on each side, he placed them over the ends of both aisles, which allowed for

Architect's drawing, made in the mid-14th century, for the west front of Cologne Cathedral, which came to light early in the 19th century.

57

greater scale and height, though at the price of squeezing the central section almost into insignificance. From France, too, came the technique of penetrating every horizontal with the sharp points of gables, but that vertical impulse finds here a finer consummation than anywhere in France in the great twin openwork spires, a very German speciality. They give the whole front a unique quality of lightness and dynamism. In the 1860s and 70s there was something very satisfying in the thought of building a real medieval cathedral which no one in the Middle Ages ever actually saw.

Milan. Interior looking east. The giant capitals, with their over-life-size figures in niches, would be unthinkable in any northern Gothic cathedral. Note too the elaborate tracery patterns painted on the vault.

Milan

ITALY never believed in Gothic. For whatever reason (the continuing strength of the classical tradition is usually suggested) Italian medieval churches have nothing of the soaring quality of those in the north.

Milan is the great exception. Founded in 1386 by a secular patron, Gian Galeazzo Visconti, Duke of Milan, it was a deliberate challenge to the Gothic cathedrals of France and England on their own terms. It was to be the largest church in Christendom: all of white marble, double-aisled, 500 feet long, nearly 200 feet wide. The height of the vault was to be 148 feet, only nine feet less than Beauvais. Remembering that disaster, however, the Italian masters decided to play for safety. The piers are made massively thick, the triforium is abolished, and the clerestory reduced to a series of small windows that are hardly more than openings in the wall. Instead of flying buttresses, the inner aisles function as supports by being carried up to the level of the springing of the vault, and these aisles are buttressed in the same way by the outer aisles, allowing them too only meager clerestory windows. To give the aisles clerestory windows at all recalls Bourges, but the whole character of Milan is different. In spite of its height the building is so wide that all vertical feeling is lost. And because the clerestory windows are so small, the main lighting has to come from the tall windows of the outer aisles, again forcing the attention downward and leaving the upper parts unemphasized.

How far all this was intended when the foundations were laid is doubtful. The original architect must have been Italian, but it soon became apparent to the Duke's building committee that he was not expert enough to carry through such a project. They decided to ask advice north of the Alps, and for many decades a succession of leading architects (from Paris, from Bruges, from Normandy, from Gmund, from Ulm) came to Milan, examined what had been built, criticized it, were occasionally put in charge of it, but all eventually quarreled with the committee and left.

In spite of its multiplicity of architects, the final result is surprisingly consistent, and is unlike anything in the north as in Italy. The exterior lacks any dominating feature (there are no towers or spires) but to compensate for that it is covered with a bewildering profusion of ornament. Over buttresses and walls runs a

Milan Cathedral: 14th-century Italy's answer to French Gothic, built of once-gleaming white marble. Every buttress and pinnacle is covered *with lace-like ornament. The west front, with its classical doors and windows, dates from the early 19th century.*

continuous net of delicate tracery, breaking out into tall, thin pinnacles above the aisles and along the roof-line. Over the crossing rises a filigree crown carrying a golden image of the Virgin. Most amazing of all are the very large, six-light windows of the choir and transepts. Their rings of spiral tracery carry the French *flamboyant* style to a new peak, and look almost as if they could revolve like Catherine wheels.

By 1500 the cathedral was virtually complete except for the west front, which (after the fashion of Italian west fronts) was left un-finished until the 19th century. To go through this dry, Neo-classical façade into the dim and mysterious interior is like entering a cavern in a marble mountain. The great piers lose them-selves in darkness, and one is hardly aware of perhaps the most unusual feature of the whole building, the capitals made up of over-life-size human figures in canopied niches.

Florence

FLORENCE Cathedral stands on the site of a Romanesque cathedral dedicated to St Reparata, of which the baptistery survives, a major building in its own right, and made more so by the arts that have been lavished upon it – the dome mosaics (begun *c.* 1300), sculpture by Donatello and Michelozzo, and the three famous pairs of bronze doors, by Andrea Pisano and Ghiberti.

Work on the new cathedral was begun shortly before 1300 and dragged on until 1418, when everything was built except the dome over the crossing. During those 120 years the scale had become progressively larger, but the style had remained more or less the same: Italian Gothic at its bleakest and barest – wide arches with few moldings, small windows, large areas of wall. The exterior is given more variety by the traditional Tuscan veneer of polychrome marble. The crossing, a huge octagon over 138 feet in diameter, was potentially as exciting as that of Ely (see p. 24). The problem that faced the authorities in 1418 was how to cover it, how to build an octagonal vault so far above the ground and so wide in span. Vasari tells some amusing stories of the desperate expedients that were considered. One man suggested filling the whole interior with earth in which coins would be buried. The vault could then be safely constructed and the earth taken away free of charge by

Detail of the Baptistery doors, designed by Ghiberti in 1422. The gilded bronze reliefs tell stories from the Old Testament.

Florentines looking for the money! When the young architect Filippo Brunelleschi put forward a scheme for building a huge dome without centering (i.e., using only scaffolding attached to the building itself) he was widely regarded as a lunatic.

His success was due to two things: first, his thorough mastery of established Gothic methods, for his proposal was in essence a very grand eight-part vault, pointed in section and supported on ribs; and second, his unprecedented knowledge of ancient Roman techniques of brick building, which he had studied in detail in Rome itself. These involved laying bricks in a herringbone pattern so that the courses were bonded together in the process of building, without the necessity of wooden centering that had to be kept in place until the whole vault had set hard. There are in fact two domes, one inside the other. The inner one, which is the steeper in pitch and therefore stronger, carries the weight of the lantern; the outer one, which is the one we see, is closer to the more classical hemisphere (e.g. the Pantheon, Rome). The whole work, therefore, is unlike anything that either ancient Rome or the Gothic north would have produced, and it rightly entitles Brunelleschi to his reputation as the founder of a new style, that of the Renaissance.

When it came to the decorative details he looked to Rome exclusively. The niches around the base of the dome and the lantern at the very top (the latter designed by him but not built until after his death in 1446) are purely classical, setting the style which was to sweep through first Italy and then the rest of Europe during the next 200 years.

Giotto's tower – the campanile of Florence Cathedral – was partly built during his period as city architect, but certainly not wholly designed by him.

Florence Cathedral. The east end. Upon the substructure provided by the earlier choir and transepts rises Brunelleschi's superb dome.

Salamanca

SALAMANCA gives us a bonus – two cathedrals in one, the first of 1152–c. 1200, the second of 1512–c. 1600, in other words the beginning and the end of Gothic architecture. Spain, like England and Germany, began by developing an early Gothic style of its own, was then carried away by the irresistible tide of French Gothic in the 13th century, and thereafter evolved an idiosyncratic late style that is wholly independent. In the 15th and 16th centuries, when the wealth of America came flooding into Spain, many cities demolished their old cathedrals and built themselves huge new ones in the latest style. But luckily at Salamanca they simply built one next to the other and left both standing.

The Old Cathedral has the simplicity and logic that one expects from this first phase of Gothic. It is of two stories only (arcade and clerestory), with thick transverse arches, quadripartite vaults and vigorous figure sculpture on the capitals. In all this it is not very different from a church of the same date anywhere else in Europe. The east end, however, could be nothing but Spanish. The transepts do not project beyond the aisles, and over the crossing rises the Torres del Gallo, a circular tower – or should one call it a dome? – two stories high, lit by sixteen windows and crowned by an umbrella-like vault with sixteen ribs. Its exterior is equally spectacular. Every window is framed in a niche, and at the four corners are turrets acting as buttresses. The stone roof is carved with a shingle pattern like fish scales.

The New Cathedral, designed by Gil de Hontañon, is almost the last great Gothic church to have been built anywhere. In 1512 only Spain was rich enough, traditional enough and religiously secure enough to embark on a building of such a size and in such a style. In northern Europe the Reformation was rumbling on the horizon. In Italy the Renaissance had already made Gothic obsolete (St. Peter's had been begun six years earlier). Yet the sheer dimensions of Salamanca proclaim the confidence of its builders in the old order: over 400 feet long, 197 feet wide, with vaults 116 feet high.

Since the 13th century the development of Spanish Gothic had been towards greater breadth and spaciousness. Spaces became unified, without architectural divisions (though split up internally by the tall screens of the *coro*, or choir enclosure, and the metal grilles across the chapels). The transepts do not

project, and the usual apse at the east end is replaced by a rectangle, so that in plan the churches are like grids. Supports tend to be far apart: Salamanca has only eight piers throughout its length, whereas Bourges (which is not as long) has thirteen, and Wells (which is a mere 310 feet long) has sixteen. But as the scale of each member grows larger the ornament becomes more delicate. Each pier is in fact a cluster of interlocking shafts, but so tiny that it gives the impression of being one colossal fluted column; the capitals have shrunk to mere ribbon-like bands around the top; and the intricately patterned ribs of the ceiling seem to have (and indeed do have) no

structural relation to the vault, but to have been applied like lace to the fabric.

It is instructive to compare Salamanca with Milan, since both follow the same basic principle – a high central nave with clerestory but no gallery or triforium, inner aisles also with clerestories and then outer aisles (at Salamanca these are divided into chapels, but structurally they are the same). Yet the two cathedrals belong to different worlds, and the difference is one of light. At Salamanca the width of the bays allows generous windows at every level, which, with the creamy gold of its stone, seem to bring the sunshine of Spain into the midst of the building.

Above *The retablo of Old Salamanca Cathedral, installed in the 15th century. These elaborate constructions, involving in this case 53 separate paintings plus the Last Judgment at the top, are a Spanish speciality.*

Far left *Salamanca, the Old Cathedral, built in the late 12th century in the simple, sturdy style of Spanish Romanesque.*

Left *New Salamanca, built in the 16th century to a scale that dwarfs the earlier building: almost the last of the great Gothic cathedrals.*

Moscow: the Dormition and St. Basil's

RUSSIAN church architecture springs from the Byzantine tradition, and until the 18th century was practically uninfluenced by the West. Buildings were small in scale, and usually square in plan, with dark interiors divided up by screens and painted all over with figures of saints. On the exterior, instead of towers and spires they had domes, as many and as bulbous as possible.

The Cathedral of the Dormition inside the Kremlin fortress fulfills these criteria fairly completely and so seems thoroughly Russian. In fact its architect was an Italian, Antonio Fioravanti, who had been called to Moscow in 1474 by Tsar Ivan III in order to remedy the shortcomings of his local builders. Fioravanti was an engineer from Bologna, evidently ready to adapt himself to any style that was required. He was told to model his work on the 12th-century cathedral of Vladimir and did so very faithfully.

The Dormition is roughly a cube with apsidal chapels added at the east end. The cube has four tall, thick piers in the middle, dividing the interior into nine equal spaces, a common Byzantine arrangement. This interior is wholly lacking in architectural enrichment and relies on painting to give it a devotional character. Every available surface, piers as well as walls, is occupied by over-life-size saints and angels against a predominantly gold background. The exterior is equally plain. On the south side, which is the church's main façade, one sees only five wall bays, with two windows per bay, the lower row connected by a blank arcade. But the roof blossoms into a display of five gold domes – a promise of the oddly moving atmosphere within.

If the Dormition is a brilliant imitation of Russianness, St. Basil's is Russia personified, unique and inimitable. True, the model is still Byzantine. There is still a central dome surrounded by a cluster of smaller domes. But the model is a thousand years away. During most of that time Russian architecture has been isolated, has lost its feeling for organized space, has been constructed mostly in wood, has picked up the strong decorative shapes and bright colors of folk art. St. Basil's marks the emergence of a style that is neither Byzantine nor in any way European. It was built some thirty years later than the Dormition (1555–60) on the orders of Ivan III's successor Ivan IV (the Terrible). One always used to read that its architects were called Postnik and Barma, but it now seems probable that those are two names for the same man.

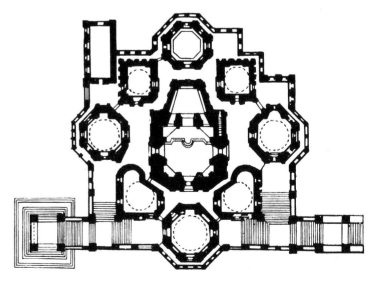

St. Basil's, Moscow, is not a cathedral in the Western sense, having no unified interior space. It consists of nine separate chapels, each surmounted by a fantastic dome and spires. The ground plan is illustrated above.

The plain exterior of the Cathedral of the Dormition, Moscow, is enriched by superb gold domes, a speciality of Russian architecture.

In spite of its fantastic appearance, the exterior of St. Basil's does carefully reflect its interior, since it is made up of nine separate, enclosed, small chapels. The main one, in the center, is covered by the strange octagonal cone that is the dominant accent from a distance, the others by the eight onion domes around it. The materials are stone for the center, brick for the rest, covered with stucco and painted. Each dome has a different design, rows of superimposed arches and sharply pointed gables being the favorite motifs. Originally the separation of the chapel roofs from the center was more clear cut, for the galleries at ground level were added only in the 17th century.

St. Peter's, Rome

IMAGINE the effect today of an announcement by the pope that he intended to demolish St. Peter's and replace it by a new cathedral in a modern style. It would not just be architectural historians and conservationists who would be upset. Yet that is exactly what Julius II decided to do in 1506, and Old St. Peter's was then twice as old as new St. Peter's is now. It was venerated as the mother church of Christendom, founded by Constantine over the grave of the first apostle, enriched with the relics of 1000 years and the bones of dozens of popes. To many it was unthinkable that such a monument should be swept away. That this actually happened is a measure not only of Pope Julius's ferocious willpower but also of the surge of self-confidence in the face of tradition that the Renaissance represented in 16th-century Italy.

For the new cathedral was to be unlike anything that Christian architecture had ever seen before. The liturgy demanded a long building, with the altar at one end and the congregation at the other all facing forward. Now Julius's architect, Donato Bramante, proposed what is called a "central-space" church; that is, a building which is symmetrical in all four directions and of which the logical climax is not the far end, to which all attention is directed, but the center, from which all the rest radiates. Certain Byzantine churches had approached this arrangement (the interior of St. Mark's is symmetrical) but had not been conceived in the same spirit, and certainly not on the same scale. Why then did Bramante propose it and the pope accept it?

The answer is twofold. In the first place, they saw St. Peter's as a huge memorial chapel, a sort of giant mausoleum, with the shrine of St. Peter in the center. The second reason is more abstract. The circle was the perfect figure, therefore a church built in the form of a circle was the perfect church, and what was perfect was closest to God. It was a view stemming from Platonic philosophy rather than from Christian worship, but it was a typically Renaissance view. The style, it went without saying, was to be classical, the vocabulary of Roman architecture with its columns, pilasters, entablature, semi-circular arches and barrel vaults which Brunelleschi had first learned a century before.

Bramante's plan was based on the combination of the circle and the Greek cross (the cross with equal arms). At the center was a large dome supported on four arches leading to the four arms, which ended in apses. In the angles between the arms were chapels providing abutment to the dome. All four vistas, and on the exterior all four façades, would have been identical. The scale was enormous—over a quarter longer than the whole Constantinian basilica. Something of the effect intended may be gathered from Raphael's painting "The School of Athens," which uses it as the background.

Julius II died in 1513, Bramante in the following year. Only the four central piers with their arches had been built. In the years that followed later popes and later architects meditated various ways of finishing the church in a way other than Bramante had intended. Raphael, who took over in 1514, was in favor of returning to a longitudinal plan by ex-

St. Peter's, Rome. The nave, looking towards the high altar. The nave was added to

Michelangelo's cathedral by Maderno in the early 17th century.

tending one of Bramante's four arms into a long nave of five bays. Antonio da Sangallo in 1536 went back to the central-space plan but proposed an elaborate two-towered façade on the entrance side (a fine wooden model of his scheme survives). But very little was actually done. Drawings of the period show Bramante's four arches towering over the still-standing nave of Old St. Peter's. In 1546 Sangallo died and Pope Paul III appointed Michelangelo.

Despite his advanced age–he was 72–Michelangelo threw himself into the task of finishing St. Peter's with characteristic energy. He decided to reverse all the previous changes of plan and to go back to Bramante. "Whoever departed from Bramante," he said, "departed from the truth." But it was Bramante drastically simplified. Each successive architect had realized that Bramante's piers were not strong enough to support the dome that he envisaged.

Michelangelo enlarged them to massive proportions—60 feet thick (compare this with, say, 12 feet for the piers of the Ely octagon). The walls were thickened correspondingly, and a monumental portico was planned for the entrance. All the elements are on the same giant scale. The pilasters are 83 feet high and their entablature 20 feet. The vault is 150 feet above the pavement, and the interior of the dome rises to 325 feet. This dome, begun by Michelangelo but only built, to a slightly modified design, after his death in 1564, is (like Brunelleschi's at Florence) double, with an inner and an outer skin, both consisting of stone ribs and brick infilling. In spite of all Michelangelo's precautions, the ribs had a tendency to spread outwards, and ten iron chains have been fixed around the base at various times.

The old nave was not pulled down until 1606. A committee under Pope Paul V decided not to proceed with Michelangelo's façade but—after all—to build a conventional nave, a decision which every lover of architecture regrets because the dome no longer dominates either the interior (until one has walked almost the length of the nave) or the exterior (except from a distance). The designer was Carlo Maderno, whose work was competent if uninspired. The nave is of three bays, barrel-vaulted and lit by openings at the sides of the vault. The aisles, unusually, are lit by small domes hidden on the exterior behind screen walls. Maderno's façade, an affair of giant columns, entablature and an attic surmounted by statues, is distinctly weak, though it might have been improved by the two towers which he planned but never built.

The man whose personality is, after Michelangelo's most strongly imprinted on St. Peter's has not yet been mentioned: Gianlorenzo Bernini. To him are due the glorious Baroque *baldacchino* immediately under the dome and over the shrine of St. Peter; the *Cathedra Petri*, the symbolic throne of papal authority; the statue of Longinus against one of the piers of the crossing; and—in front of the façade—the magnificent oval Piazza S. Pietro, with its rows of Tuscan columns reaching out from the church and embracing the City and the World.

St. Peter's from the Vatican. On this side, not normally visible to the public, Michelangelo's exterior elevation can be appreciated and his dome seen without the intrusion of the long nave.

Bernini's Cathedra Petri, "The Throne of Peter"—the symbolic expression of papal authority, an authority conferred by the Holy Spirit in the shape of the dove.

The west front of the Lateran, added in 1735. The giant columns and pilasters are Neo-classical in spirit, but the gesticulating statues on the skyline look back to the Baroque.

The Lateran, Rome

THE church of S. Giovanni in Laterano was another Constantinian basilica of roughly the same size and style as Old St. Peter's. Like St. Peter's, after 1000 years or so it was thought to be too old-fashioned and was brought up to date, not however by complete demolition but by encasing the old work in the new (rather as the Norman nave of Winchester had been encased by William of Wykeham). Finally, again like St. Peter's, it was given a grandiose façade by a less brilliant architect that effectively disguises what lies behind it.

Of the original Early Christian nave only two large granite columns at the east end remain. But the baptistery, which stands separately a few yards to the south-east of the choir, is a valuable survival from the early 5th century. It is the oldest baptistery in Christen-

dom, the prototype of numberless later baptisteries (e.g. Florence). It consists of a two-storied octagon resting on porphyry columns. The font, for complete immersion, was in the middle.

Like every Roman church, St. John Lateran accumulated its treasure through the ages: the apse mosaics about 1290, the huge *baldacchino* over the altar in 1370, several papal tombs and a coffered ceiling in the mid-16th century.

In 1643 Pope Innocent X resolved to transform the old building into a church more worthy of the Counter-Reformation. His architect was Francesco Borromini, Bernini's rival, a less attractive man but a greater architect. Borromini seized his opportunity with both hands, proposing far more than the pope was prepared to sanction. He was not allowed to rebuild the whole church; he was not even allowed to build a new vault to the

*The nave, after Borromini's remodeling of the
1640s. He filled in every other arch, added
statues in niches and redesigned the clerestory.*

nave. All he could do was remodel the existing
walls and turn Early Christian space into
Baroque space.

He began by filling in every alternate arch.
Thus what was formerly an open hall, which
could be taken in as a unity by the eye, became
a confined room with openings leading to
undefined spaces beyond. Then he abolished
the old horizontal progression (the lines of
capitals, arches, cornices) by placing strong
vertical accents, giant Corinthian pilasters, to
fill the whole height of the wall.

The arches into the aisles are treated very
definitely as openings in a solid wall, not as
members of an arcade. Inside the arches,
instead of demi-columns or pilasters, are
strange forms like the stems of plants, almost
buried in the wall and tightly enclosed in
frames. Above them the clerestory windows
seem to thrust up through the entablature of

the giant order. At the west end Borromini
chamfered the corners slightly, closing the side
walls in upon the door on his own principle
that "the corner is the enemy of all good
architecture." In this nave of St. John Lateran
he was working within strict limits imposed
from outside, but he stamped his personality
upon it none the less ruthlessly.

Some hundred years later (1735) the church
received its present west front. Its architect,
Galilei, was the winner of a competition in
which twenty-three architects took part. He
had spent some time in England, and one can
perhaps see in this design the influence of Sir
John Vanbrugh. Certainly it turns its back
upon the emotional turmoil of Baroque, and
establishes a coolly correct classical grandeur.
Since that time the only addition has been the
extension of the choir in 1885, though the apse
with its mosaics was moved back intact.

St. Paul's, London

HAD there been no Great Fire of London, St. Paul's would be quoted today as a parallel to the Lateran—an ancient church transformed almost beyond recognition in the Renaissance. As it is, its fate was closer to that of St. Peter's.

Old St. Paul's was among the most splendid of English medieval cathedrals. It had a Norman nave, an Early English choir, a Perpendicular chapter house, and for a time a spire 489 feet high. But by the 17th century a great deal of its glory had already departed. In 1561 it had been severely damaged by fire and the spire destroyed. Under Charles I the parts west of the crossing were found to be in need of urgent attention, and no less an architect than Inigo Jones refaced the whole of the nave and transepts in Renaissance style, with classical doors and windows and scroll-buttresses copied from the Italian Baroque. At the west end he built a portico of giant

Corinthian columns which ranks among his most ambitious and successful works. After the Restoration the state of the fabric continued to give anxiety; Christopher Wren proposed a classical recasing of the interior to match Inigo Jones's exterior and the replacement of the crossing tower by a dome not vastly different from the one he eventually built. But of course, when the embers had cooled on September 8, 1666, all such schemes had become superfluous, and the way was open for an entirely new cathedral, the first to be built *de novo* in England since the foundation of Salisbury 440 years before.

The design of St. Paul's evolved in Wren's mind over a period of many years, undergoing many changes in the process and suffering some painful compromises. But from the very first one feature was constant and dominant: the dome. Since the building of St. Peter's, domes had been almost an obsession with architects. Wren never visited Italy, but he certainly knew St. Peter's from books, and he did see the latest experiments in Paris in 1665.

After a hesitant and abortive first design, Wren in 1673 produced a second that remained his favorite—that embodied in the Great Model. One is immediately reminded of Michelangelo's scheme for St. Peter's: it is a Greek cross with four equal arms (the west one prolonged by a portico) opening off a central domed space, but the arms are here connected by four *concave* walls, a novel and beautiful idea with no existing precedent. One can only regret, with Wren, that it was never built. But the pressures that obliged Maderno to add a nave to Michelangelo's St. Peter's obliged Wren to do the same to St. Paul's. The third plan (the Warrant Design) is not fundamentally different from that of a medieval cathedral—nave, transepts, choir—but Wren was at least able to retain his domed crossing which (like the octagon at Ely) embraced not only the width of the nave and transepts but that of the aisles as well. His west front was closely modeled on Inigo Jones's, but his dome was a very odd combination of dome and (wooden) steeple. Luckily, he was able to modify his ideas as building went on, and the final result, the present cathedral, is an improvement on the Warrant Design in almost every respect.

Below left *St. Paul's from the south. From here the relationship between the dome and the solid walls on which it seems to rest is seen to good advantage.*

Below *Old St. Paul's, as re-cased by Inigo Jones. He gave the nave classical windows and provided a grandiose Corinthian portico, which Wren clearly remembered when he designed the Great Model.*

The dome, to begin where Wren's thoughts always began, is a superbly original conception – more dynamic than Bramante's, more placid than Michelangelo's. From outside it is divided into four stages: a drum with Corinthian columns supporting a balustrade; a second, smaller drum with pilasters; a ribbed dome; and a stone lantern surmounted by a cross. From the inside one sees a circular colonnade (the Whispering Gallery) corresponding to the drum; then the dome, with its Thorndyke paintings; and at the apex a circular hole through which light is admitted from the lantern. Relationships between outside and inside, however, are not what they seem. There are in fact three domes, and the most important one is invisible. It is a brick cone rising from the base of the larger drum and tapering to support the lantern, which rests entirely upon it. Inside this, and reaching only about half its height, is the inner dome of brick; outside it is the outer dome of wood and lead; neither of them bears any weight but its own.

The task of supporting the dome's tremendous thrust exercised all Wren's skill. (One has to remember that no dome had ever been built in England, let alone one of this size.) It rests upon eight piers. In the Great Model, and still in the Warrant Design, the arches between these eight piers were of the same span, four opening into the nave, choir and transepts, the

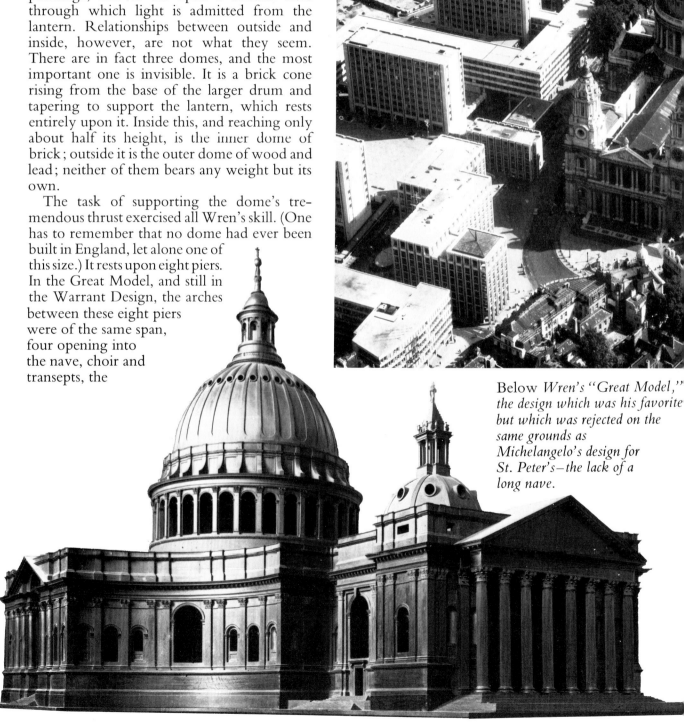

Below *Wren's "Great Model,"*
the design which was his favorite
but which was rejected on the
same grounds as
Michelangelo's design for
St. Peter's – the lack of a
long nave.

other four opening diagonally into the aisles. Now, in building, Wren found himself obliged to make the piers thicker than he had intended. To enlarge them equally in all directions would have meant a narrower nave and choir; he compromised by narrowing the aisles only, with the result that the eight arches are no longer equal. He tried to disguise this by making them rise equally high, but when one looks closely one sees that those in the diagonals are really segmental arches, posing as semi-circular ones by being extended in relief *over* the piers, not between them.

(At this point one begins to realize that a certain amount of deception has gone into St. Paul's, and moralizing critics have in fact blamed Wren for these subterfuges. This is to confuse ethics with aesthetics. In art, the contrast between appearance and reality has no meaning. Anyway, there is one more trick to come.)

The structural system of nave and choir at St. Paul's is basically the same as that in a Gothic church, except that shallow domes replace the vaults. There are two stories—an arcade, with aisles behind, and a clerestory above. From outside, however, nobody sees the clerestory windows. The aisle walls are carried up to the height of the roof, so that one imagines the interior to be a vast hall of uniform height. Only from above can one see behind the screen walls, the aisle roofs, the clerestory windows of the nave, and Gothic-like flying buttresses supporting the shallow domes. Why did Wren resort to this additional sleight of hand? Partly to give extra stability to the dome, since the screen walls provide additional abutment, but mainly for the sake of dignity and scale and to create a base of sufficient gravity for the dome. And who, looking up from the east end, will say that he was wrong?

Left *Liverpool Anglican Cathedral from the north-east. Giles Gilbert Scott's design, a truly original exercise in the Gothic style, takes superb advantage of its dramatic site.*

Right *St. Patrick's Cathedral, New York. Placed now at an unexpected disadvantage amid skyscrapers taller than itself, James Renwick's Catholic cathedral still holds its own as a building of sensitivity and character.*

Below right *Coventry. The porch connecting the old cathedral with the new, completed in 1962.*

The interior of the Catholic cathedral at Baltimore, designed by Latrobe in the Neo-Greek style.

Cathedrals in the 19th and 20th Centuries

ONE could write a history of architecture up to the 18th century mentioning nothing but cathedrals and it would not be grossly inadequate, for in the years from 500 to 1700 all that was ambitious and progressive went into ecclesiastical building. After the 18th century this is no longer so. Secular architecture, first in the form of palaces for the aristocracy, and then in the form of public or commercial premises, takes the lead. It is here that new ideas are tried out, new materials utilized, new forms invented. Church architecture, and cathedral architecture in particular, becomes tradition-bound, unadventurous, imitative. To find the reason one would have to go to the history of religion rather than of art.

The last pre-1945 cathedral to be a "modern" building was the Catholic cathedral of Baltimore, in the United States, by the English emigré architect Benjamin Latrobe. Compared to the cathedrals we have discussed hitherto this is distinctly minor. Latrobe's style is Neo-Greek, the fashionable style of 1807 when the cathedral was begun, which implies no more than that the ornamental vocabulary is derived from Greece, as Renaissance vocabulary had been derived from Rome. Latrobe had looked at Wren's St. Paul's more than he had at any Greek building. The traditional cruciform church with a domed crossing is still recognizable, but the dome has expanded to embrace almost the whole church, the choir and transepts have shrunk to mere vaulted recesses, and the nave is reduced to a two-bay vestibule. All these open into the central domed space by segmental arches, with smaller semicircular arches between them. Ornament is confined to shallow moldings, incised lines and coffering. When it was dedicated in May, 1821, it was one of the most original cathedrals in the world, an attempt to meet the needs of a young society in a style only remotely based on historical models. It might have heralded a new movement in cathedral building, with a rich heritage.

What actually happened was the Gothic Revival. We have seen something of the way this was developing in the completed west end of Cologne Cathedral. Gothic, ran the theory (first put into words by the English architect A. W. N. Pugin), was the style of the great age of faith, so it was the true and only "Christian" style. In order to revive faith we must revive Gothic; we must study medieval buildings deeply and imitate them as closely as we can.

Frederick Gibberd's Catholic Cathedral of Liverpool is clearly influenced by Brasilia. Light enters through the cupola at the top and chapels of varied shape are fitted in between the struts. In the distance to the left is the Anglican cathedral (see p. 76).

By the mid-19th century this theory was accepted all over northern Europe, in America and in the European colonies (southern Europe clung tenaciously to Baroque, which was *its* architecture of faith). Examples are legion, and the men who designed the best of them were, as individuals, not less gifted than their medieval predecessors. But the element of pretense in their artistic credo has in the end proved fatal to their works. There is a deadness about a great Neo-Gothic church which no amount of historicist fervor can disguise. Indeed, one finds oneself looking not for what is convincingly 13th-century but for what is honestly 19th, pleased to discover beneath the assumed leather apron of the master mason the frock coat of the Victorian professional.

To glance now at a few instances. St. Patrick's Catholic Cathedral in New York provides an interesting link with an earlier chapter, for it was being built at the same time as Cologne, and its architect, James Renwick, certainly knew when he designed it in the 1850s what the new-old towers of Cologne were going to be like. Otherwise, with its mixture of national styles and its wooden vault imitating stone, it is something of a compromise, and now seems curiously miniature amid the giant towers of Rockefeller Center.

England, which had from the first been among the leaders of the Gothic Revival, produced several cathedral architects of distinction. Among these were J. L. Pearson, who designed Truro Cathedral in 1880, and the more eccentric and therefore more interesting William Burges. In 1858 Burges, together with his partner Clutton, won the international competition for Lille Cathedral in northern France with a confident and vigorous design which was, however, never built. He was luckier in 1863 when he won another cathedral competition, for St. Fin Barr's, in Cork. The style is basically that of the late 12th century in northern France, but Burges allows so many quirks of his own very quirky personality to show through (not least in the animal carvings which he also designed) that it could hardly be mistaken for a genuinely medieval building.

Some of the most ambitious Neo-Gothic cathedrals are still laboring towards completion – witness St. John the Divine in New York, begun in 1892 on a vast scale and not yet finished. It is potentially of interest, since it is a "hall church" (i.e. the aisles are as high as the nave), but its whole character has twice been drastically changed, once in 1911 when Ralph Adams Cram transformed La Forge's Romanesque-Byzantine into Gothic, and again when it was decided to replace Cram's Gothic crossing tower with a concrete dome on a drum. In England the Anglican cathedral of Liverpool has suffered similar changes of plan, though mostly at the hands of its own architect, Giles Gilbert Scott. Begun in 1904, it contains one of the few original ideas to come out of the Gothic Revival: the very tall crossing tower, open to the interior, rises above a central space which is not in fact a crossing, but the interval

Brasilia Cathedral, by Oscar Niemeyer. The floor of the cathedral is sunk beneath the ground, so that all one sees is a transparent corona of glass.

between two pairs of transepts. It is liturgically meaningless, but it produces a spatial experience which is completely in the spirit of Gothic, though entirely without Gothic precedent.

Although by 1920 even the Anglican Church had recognized that historicism was dead, it was not until after World War II that any cathedral was designed with more than a nod in the direction of modern architecture. Sir Basil Spence's new Coventry Cathedral, replacing the medieval one destroyed in 1941, was bold for its date, though as the years pass it seems to be closer to Neo-Gothic than was generally thought at the time. It is in fact a clever combination of medieval motifs, taken from diverse sources and translated into a modern idiom – tall windows filled with colored glass, a wooden canopy suggesting fan-vaulting, a huge pseudo-Romanesque tapestry by Graham Sutherland. Whether these motifs come together as a unity is debatable. What is certain is that they do not constitute a new stylistic language.

For wholly novel, wholly 20th-century ideas in cathedral building we must go to two non-European architects, the Brazilian Oscar Niemeyer and the Japanese Kenzo Tange. Both have evolved architectural solutions which, while linked to traditional forms, go far beyond them.

Brasilia Cathedral consists of twelve concrete struts, 120 feet high, shaped like boomerangs. These lean together to form a circular crown, creating a dynamic upward thrust with as much energy as the flying buttresses of Beauvais. All between the struts is glass, so that the whole building is completely transparent. Niemeyer's design can be seen as the apotheosis of the central-space church of the Renaissance–Michelangelo's St. Peter's in concrete and glass. It has been reproduced in drabber materials and with fussier details by Frederick Gibberd in the new Catholic cathedral of Liverpool, which, whatever its merits, cannot be called exhilarating. It stands on the plinth formed by the crypt which was all that was built of Edwin Lutyens' Byzantine design.

On the other side of the world, Tange's Cathedral of St. Mary, in Tokyo, was begun in 1964. Tange takes the cross shape of the traditional cathedral and magically transforms it. Imagine the four arms of a Gothic cathedral; replace the vault with glass, and make the end of each arm a sheer glass wall; then pull out the walls as if they were the sides of a tent until there are straight lines at ground level between the ends of the arms (i.e. the plan is roughly like a kite); then depress the crossing, so that these ends are actually the highest parts of the building. All this is made possible by the use of reinforced concrete in tension. The dominant effect, as at Brasilia, is of irresistible upward movement, perhaps the clearest expression of spiritual force in any architecture since the Middle Ages. Is it a sign that after 250 years the triumphant progress of cathedral building is at last to be resumed?

Tokyo Cathedral, by Kenzo Tange. We are looking at the entrance—a sheer wall of glass. Behind it the nave roof slopes downwards to the crossing, where the roofs of the transepts and the choir rise in matching arms.